China Since the
Cultural Revolution

China Since the Cultural Revolution

From Totalitarianism to Authoritarianism

Jie Chen
and
Peng Deng

PRAEGER

Westport, Connecticut
London

Library of Congress Cataloging-in-Publication Data

Chen, Jie.
    China since the Cultural Revolution : from totalitarianism to
  authoritarianism / Jie Chen and Peng Deng.
       p. cm.
  Includes bibliographical references and index.
  ISBN 0–275–94647–9 (alk. paper)
    1. China—Politics and government—1976– . I. Deng, Peng.
  II. Title.
  JQ1508.C462   1995
  320.951—dc20   94–28006

British Library Cataloguing in Publication Data is available.

Library of Congress Catalog Card Number: 94–28006
ISBN: 0–275–94647–9

First published in 1995

Praeger Publishers, 88 Post Road West, Westport, CT 06881
An imprint of Greenwood Publishing Group, Inc.

Printed in the United States of America

The paper used in this book complies with the
Permanent Paper Standard issued by the National
Information Standards Organization (Z39.48–1984).

P

In order to keep this title in print and available to the academic community, this edition
was produced using digital reprint technology in a relatively short print run. This would
not have been attainable using traditional methods. Although the cover has been changed
from its original appearance, the text remains the same and all materials and methods
used still conform to the highest book-making standards.

Contents

China Since the
Cultural Revolution

1

Introduction: Exploring a New Approach

Since late 1976, when the Great Proletarian Cultural Revolution ended, the People's Republic of China has undergone a series of profound political changes, which had reached a turning point during the Democracy movement of 1989. These changes have challenged Western scholars to update and refine their knowledge and understanding of contemporary Chinese politics. Confronted by these challenges, however, students of Chinese politics in the West have not yet developed a theoretically complete and in-depth explanation of these ongoing changes, except for some narrative observations on the Democracy movement of 1989. Moreover, it seems even more academically frustrating that previous theoretical approaches to the study of Chinese politics, despite their sophistication, fail to provide a conceptual framework in which the nature and pattern of sociopolitical changes occurring since the Cultural Revolution can be systematically analyzed and the future of the Chinese polity can be predicted.

This book, therefore, explores a new approach to contemporary Chinese politics. Specifically, this approach will treat sociopolitical changes in China since the Cultural Revolution as representing a transition from a totalitarian regime to an authoritarian regime. The underlying notion is that changes in sociopolitical conditions cause a change in public attitudes toward the regime; consequently, a fundamental change in the public attitudes will eventually cause a change in the nature of the regime itself. Based on this framework, the basic dynamics and pattern of political changes in China since the end of the Cultural Revolution will be explored.

CURRENT APPROACHES TO THE STUDY OF CHINA'S POLITICAL CHANGES: THE TOTALITARIAN MODEL VERSUS THE PLURALIST MODEL

Political change in China since the Cultural Revolution, and especially the commencement of the post–Mao reform, has inspired many studies in the West. Among many approaches, two stand out as most central in contributing to our understanding of recent political changes in China. Both have their limitations as well as merits.

One of these approaches argues that the unique and deeply rooted Chinese culture (or tradition) has long fostered totalitarian rules of any Chinese national governments and their official ideologies; let us call this argument the totalitarian approach.[1] As C. P. Fitzgerald pointed out, this approach treats the Communist regime as a contemporary incarnation of Chinese totalitarian tradition:

The Chinese Communists, embracing a world authoritarian doctrine in place of one local to China, have enlarged the arena in which old Chinese ideas can once more be put into practice, in more modern guise, expanded to the new scale, but fundamentally the same ideas which inspired the builders of the Han Empire and the restorers of the T'ang.[2]

According to this approach, any drastic or qualitative political change is unlikely to happen in China unless the orientation of the Chinese culture can be shifted away from the preference for totalitarianism.

This approach, which is derived from a sinological tradition that underscored the uniqueness of Chinese culture, firmly embraces two major analytical propositions: (1) Chinese political culture inherently has a strong and popular preference for totalitarian rule, or "wise-and-able" monarchy (*xianming junzhu*), and (2) this culture, as the sociopolitical and psychological source of China's totalitarian regimes, has been deeply entrenched in the minds of both the rulers and the ruled for thousands of years and is unlikely to be eradicated.[3] Tang Tsou, for instance, believed that the cult of personality and obedience to authority embedded in the masses of contemporary China "derived implicit support from the previous long history of worship of emperor," which is, he said, "the cognitive, evaluative, and emotive orientations of the 'feudal' political culture."[4] While he was able to describe some of the important sociopolitical changes that resulted from Deng Xiaoping's reform program, he admitted he could not identify "the larger factors . . . which can be induced to account for the rapid collapse of the totalitarianism of the ultraleftists [in the Cultural Revolution]."[5] He argued that since Deng came into power, China "has come back from the brink of revolutionary–'feudal' totalitarianism" and "the relationship between political power and society in China is beginning to undergo a change in *direction*."[6] However, he found it difficult to specify the direction and nature of such changes.

In the same vein, after the 1989 Democracy movement, quite a few scholars tried to explain the relationship between the reforms and this political turmoil. They believed that to make any sense of the unrest, one must "recognize the massive weight of *cultural inertia* which favors the state and inhibits the growth of a vibrant civil society."[7] In other words, any possible political change in China should be viewed only within the context of the unique Chinese political culture—that is, both Confucianism and Maoism, as official ideologies in different historical stages, have "denied the autonomy of the individual and made self-sacrifice for the state the highest ideal of citizenship."[8] Some scholars working within this approach even denied the existence of "a national civil society," which could be identified as nationwide institutions, interests, and voices independent from the officialdom.[9] On the one hand, they suggested that the combination of disillusionment brought about by the Cultural Revolution and the decade of "opening" to the West had inspired a spirit of individualism among the Chinese people. On the other hand, they implied that the newly aroused individualism could not gain enough momentum to change the relationship between the ruling and the ruled classes unless the fundamental feature of Chinese culture—the preference for depending on authority—could be eradicated. The 1989 Tiananmen incident proved that the Chinese leaders, though regarding themselves as Communists, still believed that as rulers, they had divine rights to suppress popular resentment by force. The public silence after the Tiananmen incident also indicated that most of the people recognized and accepted the ultimate authority of the central government in Beijing to determine the nation's destiny.

To revise this view of culture-oriented totalitarianism, another group of China scholars recently initiated the so-called neoculturalist perspective as a variant of the former view.[10] While they have "a fascination with political culture"[11] in analyzing China's political changes similar to scholars of the totalitarian approach, the neoculturalists believe that "cultural traditions provide raw materials for political action, but not in any formulaic fashion."[12] Chinese political culture, they suggest, is multiplicate and "fluid" in nature;[13] thus, "creative deviation and breakthrough" in Chinese politics can be expected.[14] However, this approach refuses to establish any *causal* relationships between political culture and the polity; it merely acknowledges the "inextricable and interactive connections" between them.[15] Thus, the approach seems to lack vigor in finding the causes of political changes, despite its alleged comprehensive analyses of China's current political changes. In short, the neoculturalist perspective does not diverge much from the position of the totalitarian approach, because the former maintains the latter's fundamental assumption and fails to establish its own vigorous, analytical hypotheses.

Although this perspective speculates that "the events of 1989 may have fundamentally altered Chinese political arrangements," it does not indicate a specific direction for such transformation.[16]

In sum, the analysts of the totalitarian model have vigorously suggested that the sociopolitical roots of totalitarian rule in China consist of the unique Chinese political culture, which has a strong tendency toward totalitarianism. This tendency has been reflected in the whole course of China's political development, in which the people have persistently sought a single, yet perfect, authority to govern every aspect of social life instead of pursuing their own sovereignty.[17] Because these "basic cultural predispositions remain remarkably the same," analysts of this approach predict no dramatic political change (such as a transition from one type of regime to another) in the foreseeable future.[18]

The other dominant approach to the study of China's political changes argues that, despite its ruling position, the Chinese Communist Party (CCP) has by no means achieved *totalitarian* control over the Chinese civil society since 1949.[19] Because this approach is kin to the pluralist theory (which has often been applied to the study of Western political systems), let us call it the "pluralist" approach.

Like the pluralist theory, which argues that "no single individual or group could exercise total power over the whole gamut of public policy,"[20] scholars of the pluralist approach to the study of Chinese politics—whether focusing on formal bureaucratic politics or informal factional politics—suggest that, like any other political regime (especially regimes in the West), the Communist rule in China has always fostered the "competition among different [sociopolitical] components."[21] For example, those who study bureaucratic politics believe that the structure of the Chinese state is "fragmented, segmented, and stratified," which "promotes a system of negotiations, bargaining and the seeking of consensus" among bureaucratic interests.[22] As a result of the segmentation, bargaining, and consensus, policy-making and changes tend to be "protracted" and "incremental."[23] For these scholars, the CCP is but one, albeit powerful, political force, which has long been compelled to "share power with such other organizations as the bureaucracy and the army."[24]

Along similar lines, analysts of factional politics argue that "Chinese politics at the central government level has been structured largely by factions"; within the Chinese ruling elite, "no faction will be able to achieve and maintain overwhelmingly superior power. . . . One faction may for the moment enjoy somewhat greater power than rival factions, but this power will not be so much greater that the victorious faction is capable of expunging its rivals and assuring permanent dominance."[25] Moreover, this factional fluctuation causes "the zigzag course of Chinese politics."[26]

This approach implies that political changes in China could be caused by an imbalance of political powers and aroused by unfairly represented social groups, while political culture could be a less important factor in the changes.[27]

Moreover, the changes should be viewed as a process involving "all those mutually conditioning interactions that occur among elements of the polity that we are accustomed to think of as rather distinct and often as rather static."[28] For scholars of this approach, moreover, political changes in China could not be harder to understand than those in any other countries—that is, interactions among different sociopolitical groups and conflicts of various interests have constantly resulted in political turmoil. The Tiananmen incident was just one of the political crises that could lead to a greater turbulence or a depression in future China. In any sense, Chinese politics, which is no different from the politics of other countries, will continue to serve as just one of the processes of the "interactions" of political forces in the Third World (or old communist bloc) countries.

It is worth noting that, although these two approaches view political changes in China from quite different perspectives, their recent studies tend to come to quite similar conclusions, which are mostly descriptive and made in a highly speculative manner. Both agree that the political changes since the Cultural Revolution have led to "a more open and complex" society in which individuals enjoy greater freedom in striving for their own economic, cultural, social, and even political, ends "outside party control."[29] Neither of these approaches, however, clearly defines qualitatively the change in the nature of the Chinese polity since the Tiananmen incident of 1989.

To adherents of the totalitarian approach, the Chinese polity appears relatively static, and any fundamental change in the nature of the polity is unlikely, since the very Chinese political culture remains essentially the same and continues to be "singularly important in shaping Chinese politics."[30] Thus, any political change in China invariably leads to one type or another of totalitarian rule, which differ only in the "degrees of totalitarianness."[31]

While emphasizing changes in the power configuration, the pluralist approach does not delineate the direction of such changes. Changes thus become floating processes which can be best characterized on a continuum extending from decentralization and liberalization to centralization and restriction. To scholars of this approach, the current Chinese polity is so volatile that it could create any type of political system except an orthodox Communist regime. Such a view suggests a reluctance, if not an inability, to identify some of the most decisive shaping forces of Chinese politics from among the myriad factors.

These recent studies have certainly broadened our perspective on Chinese politics since the Cultural Revolution. They contribute to our understanding of contemporary China by bringing into focus the sociopolitical conditions of the changes that have occurred. At the same time, these studies have, indeed, "generated more controversy than consensus" among students of Chinese politics.[32] This study stems therefore from both our quandary on reading some of the representative studies on contemporary China and the desire to develop an analytical model that can more realistically reflect the dynamics of Chinese politics and forecast the direction of the fast-changing Chinese polity.

AN ALTERNATIVE MODEL: A TRANSITION FROM TOTALITARIANISM TO AUTHORITARIANISM

One of the greatest merits of some previous studies of China's politics seems to be their insight into the sociopolitical conditions for dramatic political changes. For example, while calling for special attention to the Chinese cultural preference for totalitarian rule, Lucian Pye pointed out that a series of social upheavals, such as the Anti-Rightist Campaign and the Cultural Revolution, as well as citizenry's disillusionment with the party's "correctness" have all "combined to . . . compel the people to worry about themselves as individuals" who should control their own destinies. While the form of the traditional "state-individual" relations remains, he observed, the structure of the relations has begun to crack.[33]

Such an observation implies that the public willingness to obey the Communist rule in exchange for a good life has been gradually altered by changing sociopolitical conditions, such as the miserable consequences of Communist rule, especially during the Cultural Revolution. Consequently, the nature of the relationship between the rulers and the ruled has begun to change. The people are no longer willing to subject their destinies to this rule, and they are beginning to demand a change in the Chinese polity, which had previously always dictated to the people. In other words, while a particular sociopolitical environment provides the basic preconditions for a change in the nature of polity, the dynamics of such a change should come from the people.

Drawing on Plato's *Republic*, for example, Gabriel Almond also argued that "the structural and performance characteristics" of a polity derives from "the values, attitudes, and socialization experiences" of the people.[34] This argument implies that changes in people's attitudes will eventually result in a change in the nature (or "structural characteristics") of the regime. In other words, changes in the former entail a change in the latter. In the face of shifting public attitudes, the leadership of a regime either voluntarily takes the initiative in reforming (as Deng Xiaoping did in the early years of reform) or is simply compelled to react in order to maintain its legitimacy. In either case, liberalization seems inevitable. Such liberalization "may not be the outcome leaders desire most but [rather] may be the outcome that is least unacceptable" for them.[35]

Based on the implications of the studies mentioned here, for our new analytical model we can safely assume that the public attitudes toward, and perception of, a polity are significantly affected by changing sociopolitical conditions, such as the consequences of the polity's rule. Furthermore, changes in public attitudes are likely to cause a change in the nature of the polity.

From this theoretical assumption, two major hypotheses can be deduced for this new, analytical model. They are: (1) if the overall sociopolitical preconditions in China, as independent variables, change significantly over a given time period, the public attitudes toward the regime will change; (2) as the public attitudes change fundamentally, the nature of the regime, as a dependent variable, will eventually change. In other words, two interrelated causal relationships are postulated here: One is between the overall sociopolitical preconditions and public attitudes, where the former is the independent variable and the latter, the dependent variable, while the second relationship is between public attitudes and the nature of the regime, where the former becomes the independent variable and the latter, the dependent variable.

Furthermore, in this study, it is assumed that the political change from Mao's era to the time of Deng's reform is a transition from a totalitarian regime to an authoritarian one. This change in the nature of the regime can be detected by looking at its varying "institutional arrangements: the manner in which political relationships are structured, patterned, and organized."[36] Samuel Huntington concisely summarized the characteristics of the "institutional arrangements" of both totalitarian and authoritarian regimes, as follows:

[A totalitarian regime is] characterized by: a single party, usually led by one man; a pervasive and powerful secret police; a highly developed ideology setting forth the ideal society, which the totalitarian movement is committed to realizing; and government penetration and control of mass communications and all or most social and economic organizations. A traditional authoritarian system, on the other hand, is characterized by a single leader or small group of leaders, no party or weak party, no mass mobilization, possibly a "mentality" but no ideology, limited government, "limited not responsible, political pluralism," and no effort to remake society and human nature. This distinction between totalitarianism and authoritarianism is crucial to understanding twentieth-century politics.[37]

To supplement the characteristics of the authoritarian system, Roy Macridis added one more—"rule by force":

Authoritarianism in its naked form is almost always associated with instruments of coercion and their pervasive use. The army, the police, and the jails or concentration camps—even outright assassination of dissenters—are ever present and constantly used.[38]

The characteristics of totalitarian regime described here are, we believe, a good match with those of the Communist rule in Mao's era: a dominant political organization—the Chinese Communist Party (CCP) that absolutely controlled all aspects of sociopolitical life, and a highly developed "official ideology"—Mao Zedong Thought that was the sole principle to which the entire society must conform.[39] As Amos Perlmutter pointed out, totalitarianism is "sustained by a combination of organization and ideology."[40] In other words, the party's absolute leadership through its capable and monolithic organizations and the indisputable official ideology were the two most mighty *pillars* supporting the totalitarian rule in Mao's era. Any change or decay in the nature of this totalitarian regime must result from a change or erosion in the two pillars. Therefore, the party's leadership (or the capability of its organization) and the role of the official ideology can be two important indicators for detecting a change in the nature of the totalitarian regime. Consequently, serious decay of both the party leadership and official ideology after the Cultural Revolution, accompanied, significantly, with a pervasive use of coercion, can be seen as indicating a transition from the totalitarian regime to an authoritarian rule.

Thus, the people's (or public) attitudes toward the regime should be measured, or at least detected, by mainly looking at their changing positions on the issues of the *party leadership* and the *official ideology*—Mao Zedong Thought—because these positions are most relevant to the nature of the regime. These changing positions have been expressed either through formal channels, such as public speeches, and the media, or through informal channels, such as private conversations and underground publications, passive boycotts, and even mass demonstrations.

In sum, the whole process of political change in China after the Cultural Revolution can be hypothesized as a significant political transition from a totalitarian regime to an authoritarian regime. This central tenet and other related hypotheses will be empirically tested through the examination of major political events from the end of the Cultural Revolution up to the present. This work, as its title suggests, will focus on the transitional period that started in the late 1970s that witnessed the end of the Cultural Revolution, the death of Mao, and the emergence of Deng as the new Party chief. This transitional period promptly ended in 1989, the year that witnessed the outbreak of the popular Democracy movement and the Tiananmen massacre. We call this period a transition because it was the link between the old totalitarian regime and a new authoritarian government. Moreover, it could be best characterized by sociopolitical uncertainty coexisting with a strong tendency toward a totalitarian rule. In addition, a series of important political incidents in 1989 signified the end of this transition, for currently in China, "'Abnormality' is no longer the central feature of political life, that is, [now, the] actors have settled on and obey a set of more or less explicit rules."[41] As discussed in the following chapters, after 1989, the Chinese polity came to settle on a set of new rules, which can be identified with an authoritarian regime.

SIGNIFICANCE OF THIS STUDY

On at least three grounds, this volume promises to make a significant contribution to the study of contemporary Chinese politics. First, it yields important findings about the *dynamics* and *pattern* of China's political changes since the end of the Mao era. It identifies the most important sociopolitical preconditions for the changes in public attitudes and establish some patterns of interactions between them. It also reveals the impact of public opinion and mass movements on the seemingly ironclad regime. Furthermore, based on our theoretical model and understanding of the nature, dynamics, and pattern of the sociopolitical changes since the Cultural Revolution, this book will make some reasonable forecasts about the future of the current polity.

Second, it is our hope that this study will add a valuable dimension to the understanding of current sociopolitical changes in China with its extensive use of primary Chinese sources, many of which have been heretofore untapped by China scholars in the West. Finally, since "the distinction between totalitarianism and authoritarianism is crucial to understanding twentieth-century politics," the work is also intended to stimulate more discussion on this topic.[42] We hope it will help illustrate this distinction and attract more interest to political transformations in the Third World in general, and the authoritarian government in China in particular.

NOTES

1. Important works in this approach include, for example, John King Fairbank, *The United States and China*, 4th ed. (Cambridge, Mass.: Harvard University Press, 1983); Lucian W. Pye, *The Spirit of Chinese Politics* (Cambridge, Mass.: Massachusetts Institute of Technology Press, 1992); Richard Solomon, *Mao's Revolution and Chinese Political Culture* (Berkeley: University of California Press, 1971); Lucian W. Pye, *Dynamics of Chinese Politics* (Cambridge, Mass.: Oelgeschlager, Gunn and Hain, 1981); Lucian W. Pye, *The Mandarin and the Cadre* (Ann Arbor: University of Michigan Center for Chinese Studies, 1988); Immanuel C. Y. Hsu, *The Rise of Modern China*, 2nd ed. (New York: Oxford University Press, 1975); Mark Mancall, *China at the Center: 300 Years of Foreign Policy* (New York: Free Press, 1984); Gilbert Rozman, ed., *The Modernization of China* (New York: Free Press, 1981); Ping-ti Ho and Tang Tsou, eds., *China in Crisis*, vol. 1 (Chicago, Ill.: University of Chicago Press, 1969); and Frederic Wakeman, Jr., *The Fall of Imperial China* (New York: Free Press, 1975).

2. C. P. Fitzgerald, *The Birth of Communist China* (Harmondsworth, U.K.: Penguin, 1964), p. 42.

3. Concerning this sinological traditions, see, for example, John K. Fairbank, *The United States and China* (Cambridge, Mass.: Harvard University Press, 1948), and also

his *China: A New History* (Cambridge, Mass.: Harvard University Press, 1992); Karl A. Wittfogel, *Oriental Despotism* (New Haven, Conn.: Yale University Press, 1957); Joseph R. Levenson, *Confucian China and Its Modern Fate*, 3 vols. (Berkeley: University of California Press, 1958–1965); and Richard J. Smith, *China's Cultural Heritage: The Ch'ing Dynasty* (Boulder, Colo.: Westview Press, 1983).

4. Tang Tsou, "Back from the Brink of Revolutionary–'Feudal' Totalitarianism," in Victor Nee and David Mozingo, eds., *State and Society in Contemporary China* (Ithaca, N.Y.: Cornell University Press, 1983), p. 55.

5. Ibid., p. 59.

6. Ibid., pp. 59, 88. The emphasis is added by these authors.

7. Lucian W. Pye, "The State and the Individual: An Overview Interpretation," *China Quarterly* 127 (September 1991): 443.

8. Ibid.

9. See, for example, Thomas B. Gold, "Party-State versus Society in China," in Joyce K. Kallgren, ed., *Building a Nation-State: China after Forty Years* (Berkeley: University of California, Institute of East Asian Studies, 1990), ch. 5.

10. See, for example, Jeffrey N. Wasserstrom and Elizabeth J. Perry, eds., *Popular Protest and Political Culture in Modern China: Learning from 1989* (Boulder, Colo.: Westview Press, 1992); and Peter Zarrow, *Anarchism and Chinese Political Culture* (New York: Columbia University Press, 1990).

11. Elizabeth J. Perry, "Introduction: Chinese Political Culture Revisited," in Wasserstrom and Perry, eds., *Popular Protest*, p. 4.

12. Ibid., p. 10.

13. Concerning the nature of Chinese political culture, see Jeffrey Wasserstrom, "Afterward: History, Myth, and the Tales of Tiananmen," in Wasserstrom and Perry, eds., *Popular Protes*, p. 273.

14. Quotation from Perry, "Introduction," p. 5.

15. Ibid., p. 10.

16. Jeffrey Wasserstrom, "History, Myth, and the Tales of Tiananmen," in Wasserstrom and Perry, eds., *Popular Protes*, p. 273.

17. See, for example, Pye, *Spirit of Chinese Politics*, pp. 6–7.

18. Ibid., p. xi.

19. See, for example, Kenneth Lieberthal and Michel Oksenberg, *Policy Making in China: Leaders, Structures, and Processes* (Princeton, N.J.: Princeton University Press, 1988); Harry Harding, *Organizing China: The Problem of Bureaucracy, 1949–1976* (Stanford, Calif.: Stanford University Press, 1981); David M. Lampton, *The Politics of Medicine in China: The Policy Process, 1949-1977* (Boulder, Colo.: Westview Press, 1977); William L. Parish, "Factions in Chinese Military Politics," *China Quarterly* 56 (October-December 1973): 667–699; and Andrew J. Nathan, "A Factional Model of Chinese Politics," *China Quarterly* 53 (January–March 1973): 34-66.

20. Thomas M. Magstadt and Peter M. Schotten, *Understanding Politics: Ideas, Institutions, and Issues* (New York: St. Martin's Press, 1988), p. 265. For a summary of

the pluralist approach, see Alan C. Isaak, *Scope and Methods of Political Science* (Homewood, Ill.: Dorsey Press, 1985), pp. 263–270; and David Truman, *The Governmental Process*, 2nd ed., (New York: Alfred A. Knopf, 1971).

21. Nee and Mozingo, eds., *State and Society*, p. 18.

22. Lieberthal and Oksenberg, *Policy Making in China*, p. 3.

23. Ibid., p. 24.

24. Nee and Mozingo, State and Society in Contemporary China, p. 18.

25. Nathan, "Factional Model of Chinese Politics," pp. 52, 46.

26. Stuart R. Schram, "China after the 13th Congress," *China Quarterly* 114 (June 1988): 179.

27. See, for example, ibid.

28. Vivienne Shue, *The Reach of the State: Sketches of the Chinese Body Politic* (Stanford, Calif.: Stanford University Press, 1988), p. 26.

29. Gold, "Party-State versus Society in China," p. 150.

30. Pye, *The Spirit of Chinese Politics*, p. ix.

31. Tang Tsou, "The Tiananmen Tragedy: The State-Society Relationship, Choices, and Mechanisms in Historical Perspective," in Brantly Womack, ed., *Contemporary Chinese Politics in Historical Perspective* (Cambridge, Mass.: Cambridge University Press, 1991), p. 271.

32. Perry, "Introduction," p. 3.

33. Pye, "The State and the Individual," p. 457.

34. Gabriel A. Almond, "The Civic Culture Concept," in Roy C. Macridis and Bernard E. Brown, eds., *Comparative Politics: Notes and Readings* (Pacific Grove, Calif.: Brooks/Cole Publishing Company, 1990), p. 42.

35. Samuel P. Huntington, *The Third Wave: Democratization in the Late Twentieth Century* (Norman: University of Oklahoma Press, 1991), p. 108.

36. Roy C. Macridis, *Modern Political Regimes* (Boston: Little, Brown and Company, 1986), p. 10.

37. Huntington, *Third Wave*, p. 12.

38. Macridis, *Modern Political Regimes*, p. 13.

39. The term "official ideology" was once used by Roy C. Macridis: see ibid., p. 10.

40. Amos Perlmutter, *Modern Authoritarianism: A Comparative Institutional Analysis* (New Haven, Conn.: Yale University Press, 1981), p. 175.

41. Guillermo O'Donnell, Phillippe C. Schmitter, and Laurence Whitehead, eds., *Transitions from Authoritarian Rule: Prospects for Democracy* (Baltimore and London: The Johns Hopkins University Press, 1986) 4: 3.

42. Huntington, *Third Wave*, p. 12.

2

Sociopolitical Preconditions for a Transition: Legacy of the Cultural Revolution

BACKGROUND OF THE CULTURAL REVOLUTION

Like any other regime established through a revolution, the Chinese Communist government had to meet a number of fundamental challenges. First of all, it had to make the transition from revolutionary violence to peaceful reconstruction, to deliver in order to establish credibility. To do so, it had to live up to its own ambition and the expectation of the Chinese people by best utilizing China's human and natural resources which, as it turned out, proved often short of the party's ambitious program of industrialization. Second, as a party guided by Marxism-Leninism, it also had to juggle with the complex interactions between its radical, and largely foreign philosophy and Chinese culture. The task of sinifying Marxism-Leninism had between painful on the party's long journey to Beijing and was not any easier after it seized power. Especially difficult was the task of fostering a new constructive relationship between its own rank and file of professional revolutionaries, who were generally not well-versed in technology, and China's largely Western-trained intelligentsia. Third, while the party and its armed forces won largely because of their moral strength, it remained to be seen if they could maintain a vigorous and clean government. In retrospect, one realizes that in the long run, it would have been virtually impossible for any revolutionary party, including the Chinese Communists, to preserve the revolutionary ideal after the conditions of the revolution had changed or ceased to exist. An artificial effort to prolong the revolution beyond its natural life would only lead to chaos, if not disaster.

It would therefore be erroneous to view the Great Proletarian Cultural Revolution as a hiatus or a sheer abnormality in the party's history, as some court historians in Beijing suggested. Rather, the Cultural Revolution merely led the waning Chinese Communist movement to a tragic climax. Because of this, the Cultural Revolution becomes a convenient starting point for our study of transition. Summarizing his career, Mao Zedong once said that he did two things during his lifetime: one was unifying China; the other was launching the Cultural Revolution. While the first accomplishment was widely accepted, the second was opposed by the majority of the Chinese people.[1]

Most experts, both Chinese and Western, now agree that the Cultural Revolution was intended by Mao to purge his major rivals, Liu Shaoqi and Deng Xiaoping, and their principal allies both in the party and in the government, such as Peng Zhen, Lo Ruiqing, Lu Dingyi, and Yang Shangkun. It was just another episode of the cruel infight that accompanied the growth of the CCP from its very inception.

Mao ascended to the top of the Chinese Communist Party at the Zunyi Conference in early 1935 on the Long March and at a critical moment in the party's fate. During the Sino-Japanese War of 1937–1945, he further reinforced his leadership in the CCP by removing the remnants of the "Returned Students Faction" and established his role as godfather of the Chinese revolution by his efforts toward its theoretical advancement. The success of his philosophy and strategic ideas (officially designated as Mao Zedong Thought at the Seventh Congress of the CCP), laid the foundation of his legitimacy which, until the founding of the People's Republic, was never challenged by anyone in the CCP.

Mao's thought, together with the party's ability to translate it into material progress were tested during the country's reconstruction following the CCP's victory in 1949. This was a test for which Mao and his followers were not quite ready. Unfortunately, while Mao and his party were largely ignorant of economics, they were nevertheless driven by their own unrealistic self-expectations which were rooted in the nation's reaction to a century of humiliation by the West as well as their stunning success in the late 1940s. In the 1950s, the new regime scored some modest success in economic recovery, price control, and foreign affairs in the context of the Cold War. Even the socialist transformation of China's agricultural sector and private industry and commerce went reasonably well due to the formidable power of the state and optimism the party managed to inspire among the Chinese people.

In the late 1950s, however, the revolution's congenital weaknesses came into play. The party simply lacked the resources to fulfill its ambitious industrialization program, and its overbearing behavior began to estrange the urban population, especially the intellectuals, whose talents the party badly needed. In a most tragic move, Mao and his party went against China's intelligentsia in the Anti-Rightist Campaign of 1957. As if to demonstrate their ability to proceed with or without the cooperation of the nation's professionals,

Mao launched the foolhardy Great Leap Forward of 1958–1959, which ended in a humiliating fiasco. The great famine following the Great Leap Forward claimed 40 million lives and severely discredited Mao's Quixotic policy of the period.

In the early 1960s, Mao was forced to retreat to the "second line" by relinquishing his presidency of the state, thus allowing his colleagues, Liu Shaoqi and Deng Xiaoping, to clean up the mess he had made. Thereafter, Mao developed personal grudges toward his junior colleagues, who were better at economics and pursued a different approach to economic development—rather than depending on the creativity and spontaneity of the masses, Liu and Deng showed great interest in orderly progress controlled by a bureaucracy. In the mid-1960s, Mao could no longer control his bitter feelings as he found his influence in the party to be waning rapidly.[2]

The Cultural Revolution was also intended as surgery on a ruling party contracted with moral cancers. Mao and the party ideologues faced the same problem that had brought the ruin of several powerful peasant rebellions in China's history, albeit in a totally different historical context. He admonished the CCP against the "sugar-coated bullets" from the enemies of the party on the eve of its victory. The military victory, he told his people, was but the first step on the "Long March" of the Chinese revolution. The ideological department of the party attempted to combat this tendency with tireless propaganda and to sustain the revolution by indoctrinating the masses, especially the younger generation, and by remodeling the Chinese society in a policy that smacked of the optimistic environmentalism of the Enlightenment in its extremes.

At the same time, the Sino-Soviet split starting in the late 1950s created the fear of "modern revisionism" in the CCP. The growing bureaucratism in the Chinese government could be easily related to such trends in the international communist movement. It is through both the internal struggle for power and survival and external conflict with the Soviet leaders that Mao developed his somewhat Trotskyite notion of the continuing revolution operating under a socialist system. There is little doubt today that Mao intended to purge the CCP of the corrupt officials in order to revitalize the ruling party.

The Cultural Revolution was also intended to overhaul China's literary and artistic circles. The Communist state, like Chinese governments throughout history, emphasized the didactic role of literature and arts. In his famous speech at the Yanan Forum in 1942, Mao dictated the role of writers and other cultural workers as servants of the people and the revolution. In the seventeen years after 1949, the communists made some effort to revolutionize literature and art in the framework of the so-called socialist realism. However, Mao and his ambitious wife, Jiang Qing, a former actress, were not satisfied with such progress, for they found China's movie screen and theatre stage still occupied by "emperors, kings, generals, and ministers" and "scholars and beautiful ladies." In a highly charged political atmosphere, literature and drama with such protagonists could be easily identified with feudalism, capitalism, and modern revisionism. Indeed, some literary works, such as the historical play *Hai Rui Dismissed from Office*[3] by Wu Han, deputy mayor of Beijing, were almost overtly criticizing Mao's raw deal to Marshall Peng Dehuai, a loyal and outspoken communist at the Party's Lushan Conference in 1959. Others, such as the "Evening Chats at Yanshan" a series of 153 short articles in the *Beijing Evening News* by party historian Deng Tuo, satirized Mao in an Aesopian manner. Chinese cultural workers, actors, playwrights, directors and writers, therefore, became the first victims of the Cultural Revolution.

Chinese education, especially higher education, was likewise problematic to Mao who claimed that it was dominated by "reactionary academic authorities." For seventeen years, the Communist regime tried to reform China's education, first by emulating the Soviet system and then by thought reform campaigns. While the ruling party aimed to build its own army of intellectuals from workers and poor peasants, it had to utilize the talents and knowledge of the people educated in the old schools, who did not see eye-to-eye with the party on all issues. Self-taught and scientifically illiterate, Mao harbored a deep distrust toward China's school system. Such an attitude reflected the sense of insecurity and inferiority of the rank and file of the CCP. A rebel himself, he expressed his censure of China's education in 1964 and accused the system of strangling talents and destroying young people.

The theoretical premises of the Cultural Revolution were summarized in the grandiose "Sixteen Points," or "Resolution of the Central Committee of the CCP Concerning the Great Proletarian Cultural Revolution," which was passed on August 8, 1966, at the Eleventh Plenum of the party's Eighth Congress. The document set the guidelines for the Cultural Revolution. It called on the party, the army, and the Chinese people to engage in a struggle against representatives of the bourgeoisie in the party and the government in order to defend the socialist cause. It also urged the people, especially the youth, to launch a frontal attack on the so-called "Four Olds," namely, old ideas, old customs, old habits, and old traditions. In a way, the document covered up Mao's personal vendetta toward his junior colleagues. At the same time, it also reflected Mao's romantic view of how Chinese society should be shaped. It was also a reaction to the Soviet model of the socialist state which, in Mao's view, had departed from orthodox Marxism-Leninism.

Though explicit in spirit, the goals and means of the Cultural Revolution were not well-defined and became even vaguer as events unfolded and got out of hand. Mao's cohorts stumbled along while the great leader himself seemed to become fickle as he became physically infirm. In fact, the premises of the document were totally discredited when the Cultural Revolution came to a conclusion.

THE UNPRECEDENTED POLITICAL UPHEAVAL

In retrospect, the Cultural Revolution was a great gamble on the part of Mao Zedong who seemed to have few trump cards in hand. In his famed big-character poster "Bombard the Headquarters," he called on the party and the people to round up the so-called capitalist roaders both in the party and in government, in order to prevent a capitalist restoration. Almost overnight, government everywhere was paralyzed. Since Mao never clearly defined the term "capitalist roaders," 94 percent of officials at and above the vice-ministerial level were attacked and removed from their positions. An overall 80 percent of CCP officials were assaulted and 60 percent were stripped of their power. In some provinces, the number of persecuted cadres amounted to a half million.[4]

It is still amazing today to see how, in a few weeks, the capitalist headquarters, i.e., Liu and Deng were disarmed. Liu Shaoqi surrendered almost without resistance, and Deng Xiaoping was disgraced before he could react.[5] Many officials, including some at the center of the power, found themselves at a total loss in front of this unprecedented turmoil.

However, the most persecuted group was not the cadres, most of whom were rehabilitated (*jiefang*) and incorporated into the revolutionary committees in the early 1970s after acknowledging their wrongs and pledging their loyalty to Mao's line. Often referred to as the "ten years of catastrophe," the Cultural Revolution unleashed the most destructive power in human experience. In the mass frenzy to rid the revolution of its enemies, it created the greatest reign of terror China had ever seen. People labeled landlord, capitalist, or counterrevolutionary were the easiest targets of political cleansing. Even individuals with overseas connections, such as relatives in Taiwan and Hong Kong, were singled out for suspicion of espionage.[6]

The cruel politics of the Cultural Revolution called forth everybody's instinct for survival. The infight became nasty when officials attacked each other for simple self-preservation, with some collaborating with the mass organizations in order to stay in power. Such chaos relentlessly exposed the moral fragility and ideological vulnerability of the CCP apparatus. Big-character posters brought to light serious corruption in the party, which would otherwise have remained unknown to the public. Numerous stories about officials' extravagance and debauchery permanently marred the reputation of the CCP. In short, the party's image of an invincible army evaporated in the tumultuous tragicomedy of the Cultural Revolution.

The tribulations of the mass campaign undoubtedly changed the nature of the ruling party, but nowhere near as much as what Mao had wanted. Most officials were reinstated after 1970 in the three-in-one revolutionary committees (consisting of old, middle-aged, and young cadres), as Mao found most of his early followers indispensable. The party apparatus below the provincial level survived especially well since it posed no threat to the power center. In the early 1970s, except in a few places, old bureaucrats held the line following the initial shock. They developed immunity to Cultural Revolution ideology and learned to change their colors quickly for purposes of self-defense. In fact, they helped thwart Mao's initiatives and deterred the radicals' offensive by checking the growth of local rebels. No longer caring for the purity of their ideology, many simply clung to their power and prestige with greater skill and determination than ever before.

The collapse of central control further exposed the institutional weakness of the political system. Prominent in this period was the complicated tug-of-war between the conservative faction of the CCP and the rebel cadres. As political upstarts of the Cultural Revolution, the power of the latter depended on the influence of Mao and the Central Cultural Revolution Group and on the existence of rebel organizations. After the Lin Biao Affair of 1971,[7] Mao obviously aimed to keep a balance between the moderates and radicals. The restoration of the old official corps, however, directly went against the premises of the Cultural Revolution and threatened the position of the rebel cadres who had to take advantage of every opportunity to resist the counteroffensive of the moderates. Ideologically they still held the trump card, but politically, they were on the defensive. In the end, the old-timers prevailed and the rebels who were "heavily reliant for their success on patron support and the opportunities provided by mobilization politics," were disarmed and disbanded, with few exceptions.[8]

By going against the political establishment, Mao put his own career on the line. In fact, the mass psychology of the Cultural Revolution evolved around the charisma of a supreme leader, and Mao's personality helped define the upheaval. With the aura of both an emperor and a messiah, Mao was able to appeal to the masses of young people directly. To bypass the political machine, his only weapon was ideological supremacy and his personal nimbus which the party had willingly accepted in order to maintain unity. The Cultural Revolution suddenly exposed the party and the nation to an unpredictable future. The cult of Mao rose naturally, both as a result of the vigorous promotion by the official organs and due to the psychological need of the masses to create a maximum sense of security in a time of the greatest uncertainty. The frenzy, featuring the "little red book" and the "red sea" (walls were painted red for quotations from Mao) turned politics into a surreal drama. In a highly uncertain political situation, many individuals would vie with one another in their leftism simply as a measure of self-preservation. Large-scale rituals such as the prevalent "loyalty dance" also created a type of psychological orgy in which the masses who were suspicious of their fellow citizens, could establish some sense of camaraderie. Ritualistic practices such as the prayer-like pledge before each meal and the report before bedtime were laughed at, but only in secrecy. On the whole, the cult of Mao did more damage to the great leader than most innovations of the Cultural Revolution since it ran counter to the ideal of "scientific socialism." Thinking citizens could easily find parallels in Nazi Germany and Stalinist Russia. Mao seemed vaguely aware of this when he tried to stop the craze and denounced Lin Biao's genius theory in the summer of 1970.[9] However, it was too late for him to wash his hands of it.

The Cultural Revolution was marked by the divisive power of the "continuing revolution," which occurred through the formation and rivalry of the so-called revolutionary rebels, i.e., mass organizations that emerged in late 1966 and replaced the Red Guards after 1969 in the urban areas. From early 1967 on, rebel groups all over the country, with blind energy and fuzzy political ideals, began to battle each other for spoils and power. As the fighting intensified in 1968, 1969 and 1970, China witnessed some of the most horrifying massive slaughter in its modern history. Rival factions stormed lightly guarded arms depots, seized arsenals, and attacked sympathetic PLA barracks for weapons and ammunition. The fierce battles in the provinces of Sichuan, Shanxi, and Hunan are well known. In Sichuan, for example, fighting ravaged both Chengdu, the provincial capital, and Chongqing, the largest industrial center of southwest China. Due to the mutual hatred between the heads of the provincial revolutionary committee, Liu Jieting and Zhang Xiting, and the field army, commanded by General Liang Xingchu, the province experienced a chaos such as it had not seen since the turn of the century. No one can tell for sure how many buildings were destroyed under bombardment and how many people died in the sultry summers of 1967 and 1968. It is still more difficult to gauge the motives of the fighting personnel on both sides. It must have been a thrilling experience, for example, for members of the Fight-to-the-End (*Fandaodi*) faction to post and broadcast an ultimatum to the commanders of the 54th Field Army, pride of the PLA, demanding unconditional surrender. Chongqing, a city with dozens of arsenals, was an ideal place for warlike youth. Hundred of lives were lost and whole streets were demolished. The fighting must have satisfied the ego of some and provided a channel for the energy of many high school students. In Shanxi, fighters on both sides reenacted the revolutionary war by not only practicing mobile warfare but actually dressing up like the *Laobalu* (the Eighth Route Army during the Japanese War). For months, city dwellers were subject to the mercy of warring bands. The result was total apathy and hatred toward the self-proclaimed heroes.[10]

However, it is the story from Guangxi that most terrifies people. Fighting broke out between the radical April 22 groups and the conservative Great United Command. Both sides used heavy weapons, inflicting casualties on each other by the thousands. In 1969, local rebels executed thousands of their enemies in the most cold-blooded manner. Cannibalism became a political ritual through which mad mobs maintained their solidarity. The story was only exposed recently by Zhen Yi, a Chinese dissident writer in exile.[11] Mao aimed to achieve great order (*dazhi*) through great disorder (*daluan*). But in the end, such revolutionary experimentation hurt all sides concerned. Ultimately no one, not even Mao himself, was the winner.

Before the end of the Cultural Revolution, most fighting factions had been disarmed by the PLA with the cooperation of the local governments. In fact, many rebel leaders with divergent thinking were combed out in February 1967 with Mao and Zhou Enlai's endorsement. The swashbuckling chiefs were arrested for their criminal activities in the early 1970s. After the downfall of the Gang of Four, even more were incarcerated as the gang's accomplices. The memory of such fighting would become an integral part of China's national psyche. For officials who watched helplessly on the sideline, the very mention of those years must be chilling. That is why the post–Mao Chinese leadership has been able to convince many citizens of the need to prevent the Cultural Revolution from recurring.

One key to Mao's temporary success was his control of the People's Liberation Army through Marshall Lin Biao. The military stood behind Mao when he removed Liu Shaoqi and Deng Xiaoping from office; but when nationwide civil strife developed, the attitude of the PLA was much more complicated and ambivalent than many had expected. In 1967 Mao asked the military to support the "left factions" all over the nation. With few exceptions, however, the military establishment either openly or covertly sided with the conservative factions who turned "left" overnight when the term conservative faction (*baohuang pai*) became a stigma. In retrospect, it was obviously much easier for the generals and officers of the PLA to identify with the party apparatus because of its conservative orientation. Politically moderate, the military had little interest in backing up the real rebel groups. Moreover, in 1967 and 1968, when Mao became concerned with the escalation of factional fighting in many cities, the military in many provinces assumed a neutral position between the warring factions in order to foster a "great alliance of all revolutionary factions" which, more often than not, frustrated the misguided rebels.

In many localities, the field armies and local forces had their own clients among the fighting rebels and allies in local governments. The already highly politicized PLA barely refrained from actual fighting. Some generals, such as Chen Zaidao, commander of the Wuhan military region, actually defied the authority of the Central Cultural Revolution Group by detaining its members. Only Mao and Zhou were able to coerce the recalcitrant general back into line. In Xining, capital of Qinghai province, solders fired deadly volleys into crowds of rebels, killing hundreds.[12] To avoid a new warlordism, Mao had to shuffle the military units around, and in 1973, commanders of all but three military regions were transferred.[13]

Although at the Ninth Congress of the CCP the military seemed well-entrenched in the party and the revolutionary committees from the provincial to the county levels, structural damages had been inflicted on the military. A purge by the radical leadership shook the PLA high command. The rise of Lin Biao and his subordinate generals in the former Fourth Field Army Group created jealousy among generals of other field army groups, and Lin Biao's sudden downfall in 1971 likewise was followed by the disappearance from prominence of quite a few generals, especially those from the Fourth Field Army group. The removal of Lin Biao contained the growing power of the PLA but did not end Mao's problem with the military. Neither did it resolve factional struggle in the PLA. It only led to the rise in the system of Lin Biao's major rivals, whose loyalty to Mao was not ideological but political.

Economic development was not a major concern of Mao when he launched the Cultural Revolution. But the Cultural Revolution compelled the Chinese government to improvise policies to prevent China's economy from total collapse. Radical leaders wanted to release the tremendous potential of the Chinese people, especially the working class through political indoctrination. "Promote production by making revolution" was the catch phrase of the day. The Daqing Oil Field and the Anshan Steel and Iron Company were promoted as examples of self-reliance and models of revolutionary spirit translating into greater productivity. News media, and the performing arts especially, dramatized the experience of Daqing which shattered the Western myth of China as a petroleum-poor country.

Unfortunately, models like Daqing were but orderly oases in a sea of chaos, with little relevance to reality for millions of Chinese workers in the cities. Overall, the government's industrial policy during the Cultural Revolution achieved only limited success, except for isolated cases where production was barely maintained at the pre-Cultural Revolution level. Prodoctivity in the nation's key industries such as steel and machinery steadily fell, first because of the decapitation of the managerial corps, then because of the mutilation of its technological personnel, and finally because of an ultra-left policy that turned the factories into battlegrounds of class struggle and fortresses for factional fighting. The total loss was staggering: "During the decade of upheaval, the loss of national income amounted to 5,000 billion yuan, or 80% of the total investment in infrastructure constructions and over the total fixed national assets in the past 30 years."[14] Between 1974 and 1976 the nation lost about 10 billion yuan in the total value of industrial output and 40 billion yuan in state revenue, which brought the whole economy to the brink of collapse.[15] A province-by-province analysis of industrial performance reinforced this conclusion: "shortages of raw materials, disruptions in transport and work stoppages were highly correlated with, and undoubtedly caused by, political disruption."[16]

One exception to China's general economic stagnation was the development of local, and especially rural industries in the early 1970s. The policy reflected Mao's idea of industrial decentralization and the "walking-with-two-legs" approach. It was a viable alternative to the centrally controlled, and ineffective, state industry. Capital raising, operation, and marketing for such enterprises were localized and geared to meeting the needs of local industrial development. Recent studies have raised reasonable doubts about the profitability of such enterprises. Obviously due to inexperience, a great number of such enterprises were operated at a loss, and there must have been tremendous waste of human and material resources. The real significance was many of these enterprises survived at all and in some regions (especially in the lower Yangtse valley and the Pearl River Delta), they became the starting point of the post–Mao economic reform. The local and rural enterprises turned out a generation of managerial personnel who were equipped to lead their enterprises to readjust to changing circumstances after the Cultural Revolution. It is not only because of foreign investment that the coastal areas prospered in the post–Mao era. Ironically, the chaos of the Cultural Revolution laid the groundwork for economic growth in provinces such as Jiangsu, Zhejiang, and Guangdong.

The peasantry has always been a silent and docile group in Chinese society. The peasants were good subjects of the emperors for centuries except when they were struck by severe famine and abused by government officials. They put up with the collectivization of agriculture, and especially the people's commune, although not without complaints. With memories of the great famine years of 1959–1961 still fresh, China's farmers showed little interest in what was happening in the cities during the Cultural Revolution. Mao and his associates wanted to leave the farmers alone, apparently because they knew what jeopardy the country would be in if the farmers became mobilized, and also because the countryside had lost the importance for the ruling party. The city was the stage, not the countryside.

However, the Cultural Revolution did radiate into agricultural areas. Propaganda aimed at forming a new peasantry recharged the politics of rural China. Neither the farmers nor the CCP apparatus were immune to the radicalism of the turmoil. Between 1967 and 1970, factional fighting spilled over the boundaries of the cities into the paddy fields. Young farmers became mercenaries for booty and enjoyment. In some localities, discontented farmers organized against local despots, although with limited success. At the local level, a reshuffling of officials, which was sometimes extended to the production brigades and teams, did take place in many areas. The pragmatic nature of the Chinese farmers, however, was able to blunt the edge of political radicalism and only a tiny percentage of rural population became heavily involved in factional fighting.

In general, Mao's agrarian policy throughout the Cultural Revolution was two-fold. First, agricultural output had to be increased to fuel the urban economy and politics. The focus of government policy in the countryside was, therefore, stability and production in support of which the government spared no effort. Second, Mao and his followers apparently wanted to turn the Cultural

Revolution into a political education campaign to further revolutionize the peasantry. The people's commune, intended as a control mechanism from its inception, helped keep China's farmers in place on the land. Guided by the theory of class struggle, local authorities organized periodic mass meetings against the former landlords and rich peasants in order to intimidate not only the "enemies of the people," but would-be troublemakers as well.

A most prominent and consistent approach was to promote the model of Dazhai, a village on the barren loess plateau of Shanxi, which seemed to have achieved ideological excellence and material abundance simultaneously. A seeming agrarian utopia, Dazhai was lucky to have a capable and devoted leadership which kept the morale of the villagers high by their exemplary role. The village also benefited from the assistance of local army units, which used large machinery to help the villagers in their land-improvement campaign. In the early 1970s, the Dazhai experience was promoted all over the country. On the whole the policy achieved some success for China's grain output increased steadily over these tumultuous years.

The victory was not without cost, though. In the first place, the experience of Dazhai, and especially its land improvement methods did not suit every production brigade in rural China. It was especially irrelevant in the south where farming techniques were nearly perfect and large-scale land improvement was unnecessary. Second, the egalitarianism practiced by the Dazhai villagers held little appeal for farmers whose memory of the man-made disaster of the early 1960s was still vivid. Not surprisingly, the majority of Chinese farmers greeted the Dazhai model with lukewarm enthusiasm. Third, while output increased, the farmers' livelihood did not significantly improve since most of the surplus was taken by the state—so much so that many local cadres, with the villagers' support, invented various ways such as keeping dual accounts, to hide the real growth. In some localities, the cadres even divided land among villagers under the camouflage of collective farming. Moreover, incessant propaganda increased skepticism among the farmers, which explains why remnants of capitalism such as a private plot of land for each farming household were never cut off in spite of the Dazhai story.[17]

Virulent radicalism was not popular, even among the rural cadres, who remembered the cost of the radicalism of the Great Leap Forward of 1958–1959 and the benefits of the years of readjustment (1962–1964). In the 1970s, especially after the Lin Biao Affair of 1971, radicalism was losing momentum, even in the cities. The Cultural Revolution radicals were predominantly urban and, therefore, never able to work out a systematic policy for rural communization. In fact, widespread weariness among rural population of collective farming resulted in a yearning for the "good old days" following the land reform in the early 1950s when farmers, with their newly acquired means of production, could control their own fate. The popularity of Deng Xiaoping's household responsibility system in the late 1970s was by no means an accident.

For millions of Chinese students, the Cultural Revolution was a painful journey on which they lost their youth and innocence. The Cultural Revolution widened the already great gap between China and the West in science and technology by abusing the talents of the younger generation. When the first Red Guard battalion was organized, it was a spontaneous creation of youthful zeal. With Mao's endorsement, Red Guards spread throughout the country almost overnight. But the "great helmsman" hardly charted a clear course of action for the youth except to allow them to improvise. At first, the destructive energy of the Red Guards was directed against the Four Olds. Youngsters destroyed hundreds of temples, burned millions of books, ransacked the homes of suspects, and confiscated the property of their helpless victims.

Before long, orderly rebellion had turned into mob activity in which the students took delight in torturing their teachers and school administrators. It was undoubtedly a thrilling feeling for many young people who would otherwise never have had the power to occupy government facilities and humiliate such high personages as ministers, governors, and magistrates. The mass uprising against the authorities was a kind of psychological compensation for the cramped lives resulting from an indoctrination in self-denial and self-sacrifice.[18] However, power is a corrupting influence and the students' power was short-lived. Many of them must have been shocked by their savagery and penitent about what they had done to their teachers and other victims. While a small number student leaders were drunk with their petty political power and warriors toying with their machine guns, many became weary and uneasy as they found that their actions were leading nowhere.

In 1968, a tearful Mao blamed Red Guard leaders in Beijing's major universities for letting him down. Worker propaganda teams were sent to college campuses and high schools to restore order. Prominent leaders fell overnight because of the great leader's displeasure, and most college students had become disenchanted enough to accept job assignments and leave the Cultural Revolution behind them. The greatest victims of Mao's whims—and circumstances, too—were junior high school and high school students. These youngsters were instrumental for Mao and his radical associates in disarming their opponents in the government, and responsible for much of the fighting in 1967–1969. Economic stagnation and pressure from the party apparatus made Mao impatient with the lawlessness in the cities and he asked the students to continue the Cultural Revolution by going back to school. When they returned to the classroom, however, youngsters found their teachers too demoralized to offer any high-quality instruction and the entire secondary education system damaged beyond repair.

The deadly blow came in December 1968 when, in another "supreme instruction," Mao called on the urban youth to go to the countryside for "reeducation" by the poor and lower-middle peasants. In 1969, 16 million unhappy high school and middle school students had to bid farewell to the cities. It did not take much insight for the students to feel betrayed. For many, this perverse decision of Mao only showed that they had been used, and eventually disposed of, by their great leader.

In the ensuing years, the real world would give them a good opportunity to reconsider many formerly held beliefs and cherished values. Youngsters from the cities were shocked by the disparity between the socialist paradise described in their textbooks and the reality of rural China. Cow dung not only bred disillusionment, it also led to revelation. Many of the youngsters endeared with the farmers. At the same time, they were also subject to the petty despotism of local officials who in general had little education.[19]

Because of their higher educational level and more sophisticated outlook, only a minority of the urban youth really received the farmers' "reeducation." Rather, they learned through their experiences and observation the results of which were a far cry from what Mao had intended. Worse still, as was later documented, in thousands of cases local officials took advantage of the city youngsters' plight, exacting money from the boys and sexually abusing the girls. As far as the educated youth was concerned, Mao's agrarian utopia became a sheer fantasy. The policy proved a failure and ended logically in total abolition, counter to the predictions of some Western observers.[20]

In unspeakable despair, the rusticated youth became the most skeptical, cynical, and rebellious social group in China. In this sense, this was a real "Lost Generation" of in Communist China. When the colleges reopened after the Cultural Revolution, they would produce the hardest-working and most conscientious classes in the history of the People's Republic. Among this group emerged some of contemporary China's best writers, including Zhong Acheng, Zhang Chengzhi and Jia Pingao, and political scientists, such as Hu Ping and Chen Kuide. These leaders would set the tone for Chinese politics within ten to fifteen years. Without the Cultural Revolution, the enlightenment in the post–Mao era would have been simply inconceivable.

During the period of 1966–1976, China's intelligentsia went through its worst crucible since the CCP came to power. In the first few years of the People's Republic, a sort of mutual trust was established between the CCP, which needed a pool of talents for peaceful reconstruction, and China's intelligentsia, who wanted to do their share for the country's modernization under an ethical government. Such trust, however, was betrayed during the Hundred Flower and Anti-Rightest campaigns of 1957, in which 400,000 people, mostly college educated, were labeled "rightists." After missing his opportunity, Mao never regained his prestige. Sensing the lack of respect from the educated elite, Mao attempted to replace them with a new generation of both "red and expert" professionals from the working class. This was far from successful due to the inherent contradictions in Mao's philosophy and the Cultural Revolution.

Mao's deep-seated bias toward formal education and the Red Guards' behavior reflected the mentality and culture of an agrarian society. Mao was heard to have boasted that the CCP surpassed the First Emperor (Qin Shihuang) in ideological inquisition.[21] In the Cultural Revolution his contempt and vindictiveness toward the educated Chinese turned into a malignant anti-intellectualism. First directed against the establishment intellectuals, the attack soon was indiscriminately directed at the entire intelligentsia. When the Red Guards attacked the Four Olds, they often trashed the most valuable things, both Chinese and foreign, that China needed for its identity and societal health. Teachers bore the brunt of the Red Guard sadism: to this day no one knows how many were beaten to death. No one knows how many books were burned to fuel cook stoves. Writers, no matter how closely they followed the dogma of "socialist realism" became the targets of the red storm. Some of the best, such as the playwright Lao She, the translator Fu Lei, and the historian Jian Bozhan, committed suicide under the unbearable physical abuse and mental pressure.[22]

But the ordeal of the Cultural Revolution became a testimony to the glorious tradition of China's educated people. In the ten hideous years, many of them were humiliated, tortured, and subjected to forced labor in the fields and factories. As a group with an intense sense of obligation, they were deprived of the right to serve their compatriots in a time when their knowledge was most needed. Many were heartbroken when they were denounced and humiliated by their students. For some time, serious soul-searching and self-criticism took place for their failure to be closer to the working people or more loyal to the party. However, there was a limit to their self-degradation, beyond which they rebelled. Knowledge and professional pride supported them, enabling them to resist the most degrading and dehumanizing situation. Liang Shuming, the well-known Chinese philosopher, is heard to have quoted Confucius as follows: "A great army could be stripped of its commander-in-chief; but a man could never be stripped of his dignity."[23] In the end, many of them found they could shrug off their suffering of the day when they retired to their shelter at night. Even among the establishment intellectuals, doubt arose as to the legitimacy of the CCP and whether Mao personified China's socialist road.

When knowledge is depreciated, professionals may feel cheapened. Professors agonized at the generally pathetic performance of the "worker-peasant-soldier students" who came to study at the colleges in the early 1970s. They passively resisted the fumbling leadership of the workers' propaganda teams. Moreover, the ineptitude of the Cultural Revolution group and its followers in academic and economic affairs only helped restore their self-esteem when, in their barracks, they could at least gloat over the power holders' stupidity. Many came to believe that sooner or later, they would be called upon to fix the enormous mess. Such pent-up desire was well demonstrated by the story of Chen Jingrun, a genius in mathematics who attacked the "Goldbach Guess" with sheer tenacity and the outpouring of talents in the late 1970s and early 1980s. On the whole, the Cultural Revolution only helped throw China's intelligentsia out of the ideological orbit of the ruling party, beyond the pull of Mao Zedong Thought. While many forsake Maoism, their patriotism would find expression in the post–Mao era.

VOICES OF DISSENT

The Cultural Revolution, though dominated by the obscurantism of the CCP, stimulated independent thinking among the Chinese people. The breakdown of the central control created a vast space for free critical thinking even though there was not a national forum for dissenting voices. Perverse policies of the central government, mass hysteria, power struggle, betrayals, plots, and all sorts of brutality shattered the people's faith in the party and its paramount leader. People found that, after all, the Communist party was a self-seeking group, that its leaders were jealous of each other, that the party's organ, the *People's Daily*, was full of lies, that rumor contained more truth than documents of the CCP central committee, and that, above all, their wise leader was actually fallible. The Cultural Revolution, in short, broadened the gulf separating the party and the people.[24]

To make matters worse, the Cultural Revolution filled the life of the Chinese people with high-sounding rhetoric that only helped magnify problems in the political establishment. The great tension between fundamentalist propaganda and a corrupt political system ignited many people's spontaneous reactions. Indeed, the Cultural Revolution "instilled in many Chinese a readiness to challenge authority and a healthy skepticism about the promises and motives of political leaders.[25] Dissenting voices were whispers in the beginning. Then they became loud enough to shock the power center in Beijing. For those who dared to think independently, the Cultural Revolution created an opportunity for intellectual growth. However, this was an extremely tortuous, and in some cases costly mental journey.

Although scholars today would characterize the Cultural Revolution as a prime example of mass manipulation by a charismatic leader, the turmoil failed to neatly follow the course charted by Mao. It was not unusual for the radicalism of Mao and the Central Cultural Revolution Group to backfire, because the extreme ideology itself contained the seeds of its negation. Once Mao's thought was extolled as the absolute truth, anyone could use its biblical quality to defy authority, including Mao himself. In late 1966 and early 1967, for example, Red Guards in Shanghai attacked Zhang Chunqiao and Yao Wenyuan, both of whom were Mao's top lieutenants during the Cultural Revolution, and kidnapped Xu Jingxian, a leading member of the Cultural Revolution faction in Shanghai.[26] In July 1967, two members of the Central Cultural Revolution Group, Wang Li and Xie Fuzhi, were detained by members of the Army of One Million Brave Soldiers (*Baiwan Xiongshi*) and soldiers of the local military in Wuhan.[27] Though they were scattered and quickly put down, such revolts exposed the vulnerability of Mao's radical line.

In 1966, when birth became a political yardstick, an obscure young man in Beijing by the name of Yu Loke circulated a pamphlet entitle "On Birth" in which he denounced the conception of "birth determinism" as reactionary. In 1967, Yu's article was declared "counterrevolutionary" by the radical leadership in Beijing, and in 1970, Yu was executed, the first martyr for freedom of speech during the Cultural Revolution.[28] Indeed, some of the victims of the reign of terror were young idealists. The story of Zhang Zhixin, a Communist woman who was excuted in the most brutal manner even after the death of Mao was well-known.[29] In 1978, the story caused such public outrage that reputedly, Deng Xiaoping had to intervene personally to stop a further expose to salvage the tottering image of the regime.

Li Jiulian, a young women in Ganzhou, Jiangxi province, was only twenty years old when she was arrested in 1969 for questioning the Cultural Revolution and attacking Lin Biao. In 1974, Li was arrested again for trying to overturn her earlier verdict. While thousands of people in Ganzhou took to streets to show their moral support, the government arrested her again with the endorsement of the radicals in Beijing. Forty other people went to jail along with her, and over six hundred people were persecuted for their professed sympathy. In December 1977, Li was sentenced to death because, even in jail, she expressed her doubt about Hua Guofeng, then chairman of the CCP, and about the treatment of Jiang Qing. Before execution, soldiers struck a bamboo stick into her throat to prevent her from shouting "reactionary slogans." A female schoolteacher by the name of Zhong Haiyuan was sentenced to twelve years in prison for openly supporting Li. Unable to stand the barbarism of the prison administration, she wrote "Down with Hua Guofeng" on the wall of her cell. She too, was executed and before she died, her kidney was removed by some medical workers to save some VIP's life.[30]

In South China, in the fertile land of Hunan, Mao's home province, an eighteen-year-old young man named Yang Xiguang was arrested and sentenced to death for writing and circulating an article entitled "Wither China?" The son of a fairly high-ranking Communist official, Yang was attracted in 1967 by the plight and grievances of the "rusticated urban youth" who had been sent to the countryside before the Cultural Revolution. His interest in this issue spurred his "Report on the Rusticated Youth in Hunan Province," with a style reminiscent of Mao's report on the peasant movement in Hunan thirty years before.[31] With sincere belief in Marxism-Leninism, Yang questioned the validity of the Cultural Revolution. In a panic, the Central Cultural Revolution Group authorized his arrest and the suppression of his organization, the Hunan Provincial Proletarian Revolutionary Alliance Committee, or Shengwulian, one of the ultra-leftist groups in China. Immature as it was, "Wither China" represented an attempt to reframe the paradigm through which the young people perceived the sociopolitical system of China. It explained the essential conflict in China in terms of a "conflict between a manipulative class of party officials intent on preserving their power and a powerless mass of ordinary people, who had been repeatedly conned into seeing the party apparatus as their champions against imaginary foes."[32]

The best known of all was a series of big-character posters and pamphlets appearing in Guangzhou in 1974, on the eve of the Fourth People's Congress. Featuring "Socialist Democracy and Rule of Law" and "The Revolution is Dead—Long Live the Revolution," the series was written by "Li Yizhe," which was a pseudonym for three young men, Wang Xize, Chen Yiyang, and Li Zhengtian. In their articles, these daring authors repudiated the "anti-democratic" aspects of the party leadership during the Cultural Revolution, as well as what they called "social-fascism." They also attacked the expanding privileges of the party and government officials. Their call for the socialist rule of law and the rights of revolutionary supervision of the masses of people over the leadership at various levels in the party and the state sounded populist rather than Marxist.[33] Seeing themselves as reformers, Li Yizhe went so far as to criticize Mao himself but continued to adhere to Marxism and Mao Zedong Thought! The publications caused such a stir in China that Mao himself was said to have been shaken by the courage of the young rebels. The campaigns to repudiate Li Yizhe launched by the provincial CCP committee of Guangdong only helped disseminate the young men's ideas which had so much resonance among the people in Guangzhou and other major cities. In the end they were silenced only by incarceration.[34]

Other dissenter groups in the Cultural Revolution included the Support Station of the United Headquarters (Zhilian Zhan) in Shanghai, which comprised intellectuals and students; the October Revolution Group (Shiyue geming xiaozhu) in Shandong; the Big Dipper Society (Beidouxin xueshe) in Wuhan; and the April 3rd faction and the Communist Groups (Gongchanzhuyi xiaozu) of Beijing University.[35] Although small in number, these organizations and individuals were nevertheless harbingers of intellectual awakening. Their existence and activities indicated the growing discontent among an increasing number of the Chinese people, especially the urban population, which was focused on the ultra-leftism of the Cultural Revolution and the duplicity of the regime.

Such sentiment came to a climax in the April 5th Movement of 1976, a spontaneous revolt of the people in Beijing against Mao and his followers. It was a showcase of the people's will and a test of the strength of those in power. Originating in the general grief over the death of Zhou Enlai, the loyal, tireless, and selfless prime minister of the government and the epitome of the republic of virtue, the Chinese people found a legitimate way to vent their pent-up feelings.

The protest was made possible by several factors. First, there was the unique stature of the late premier Zhou Enlai who, although born in a Mandarin family, came to work for cause of the downtrodden. Since the Zunyi Conference in January 1935, Zhou's loyalty to Mao never wavered. During the Cultural Revolution, he supported Mao's policy but kept a very subtle distance from Mao's radicalism. He walked a fine line between the rank-and-file of the CCP and the radicals, including Lin Biao. Without overtly challenging Mao's will, he worked diligently to patch the cracks in the party and government, and he never lost sight of China's needs beyond the politics of the Cultural Revolution. Zhou, in short, represented the more reasonable, humane side of the Chinese revolution, apart from his generally congenial relationship with China's intelligentsia. His passing away was naturally a great psychological blow to many educated Chinese.

Starting in February, scattered opposition to the radical leaders emerged in such cities as Beijing, Chongqing, Taiyuan, Nanjing, Wuhan and Hangzhou.[36] After simmering for weeks, emotions boiled over in Beijing in April, which is traditionally a season for the Chinese to mourn the deceased. The climax came on April 5th when 100,000 people spontaneously gathered in Tiananmen Square around the Monument to the People's Heroes. Demonstrators read poems and made speeches in which they denounced the perverse policy of the Gang of Four and, in effect, questioned the very premises of the Cultural Revolution. Antipathy to the Cultural Revolution was well expressed by words such as "China is no longer the China of yore, and the people are no longer wrapped in sheer ignorance" and:

You must be mad
To want to be an empress!
Here's a mirror to look at yourself
And see what you really are.
You've got together a little gang
To stir up trouble at the time.[37]

No one could have missed the message of the demonstration, least of all Jiang Qing and her associates. Thus, the April 5th movement became an excellent example of the Chinese way of attacking the living with the spirit of the dead. It was also an opportunity for many protestors to express their support of Deng Xiaoping, who was drawing fire from the Gang of Four for his effort to restore order in China's economy. The demonstration was stamped out by the municipal government of Beijing and although Deng Xiaoping had no part in this "counter-revolutionary incident," he was nonetheless removed from his newly gained vice-premiership.[38]

In late 1976, shortly after the downfall of the Gang, most people arrested in the April 5th demonstration were quietly released. Many received a hero's welcome by their colleagues, a very unusual thing when the verdict had not been openly overturned. In 1977, when big-character posters reappeared in Beijing, many called for the reversal of the 1976 verdict on the April 5 Incident. The rehabilitation of the victims of the April 5 crackdown became a prelude to the post–Mao political decompression and the return of Deng Xiaoping to power. For Deng Xiaoping and many Communist officials, the movement unmistakably demonstrated the people's will. In a sense, the popular sentiment expressed on April 5, 1976 dictated the reform policy of the Deng administration and the set the tone for CCP-intellectual relationship in the late 1970s and early 1980s.

THE CULTURAL REVOLUTION IN RETROSPECT: A BALANCE SHEET

The October coup of 1976 occurred like a miracle. Without bloodshed, the Gang of Four was arrested and the nation expectedly celebrated the "great victory." It nevertheless took tremendous political momentum to arrest and incarcerate an "empress." Although Hua Guofeng collaborated with military strongmen such as marshall Ye Jianying, the coup would not have happened had they not been sure of the overwhelming support they would receive, both in and outside the ruling party. Hua Guofeng was hand-picked by Mao for his intellectual mediocrity—to serve as a political buffer between the radical Gang of Four and moderates in Zhou Enlai's camp. "With you in charge," Mao wrote to Hua, "I am at ease." Apparently he hoped to preserve at least part of the legacy of the Cultural Revolution by such arrangement. Again Mao had miscalculated; the Cultural Revolution had created such a strong opposition in the party and among the people that no matter what precautions he took, China's political pendulum was moving to the right. Shortly after Mao's death, Hua switched to the side of the opponents of the Cultural Revolution and issued the order to arrest the Gang of Four. The trial of Madame Mao and her associates put the last nails in the Cultural Revolution's coffin and buried Mao's dream for a proletarian utopia.

Originally aimed at overhauling the ruling party, the government, the educational system and, in fact, the entire Chinese society in the name of continuing revolution under the proletarian dictatorship, the Cultural Revolution turned into what the post–Mao Chinese government called "ten years of great turmoil."[39] None of the grand objectives was achieved except that some of Mao's rivals were persecuted to death. The devastation caused by the Cultural Revolution called into question its theoretical premises and the legitimacy of the ruling party. Intended to "preserve the revolutionary spirit beyond its natural life," it only aggravated the inherent problems in the Chinese Communist movement.[40]

Smarting from the wounds of the Cultural Revolution, the new leadership of the CCP had no good words whatsoever for the "unprecedented revolution":

Practice has shown that the "Great Cultural Revolution" did not in fact institute a revolution or social progress in any sense, nor could it possibly have done so. It was we and not the enemy who were thrown into disorder by it. Therefore, from beginning to end, it did not turn "great disorder under heaven" into "great order under heaven." History has shown that the "Great Cultural Revolution," initiated by a leader laboring under a misconception and capitalized on by counterrevolutionary cliques, led to domestic turmoil and brought catastrophe to the party, the state, and the whole people. Comrade Mao . . . confused right and wrong and the people with the enemy. . . . Herein lies his tragedy.[41]

The Cultural Revolution relentlessly revealed a hard truth: Mao's thought was the revolutionary ideology of a peasant rebellion and had little relevance to China's modernization. The revolutionary ideology became especially discredited among China's intellectuals who were becoming the backbone of China's drive for modernity. Faced with such popular sentiments, the new leadership in Beijing could reestablish its prestige only by reformulating an ideology that deviated sufficiently from the revolutionary principle but did not openly repudiate it. Deng Xiaoping's Cat-Thesis is a good expression of such a philosophy;[42] economic reform to meet the Chinese people's material needs was the only way out of the political impasse.

The end of the Cultural Revolution also marked the total bankruptcy of the concept of "continuing revolution." The idea had initially fascinated many people, especially the young and adventuresome, who found a role to play in the otherwise boring routine of politics. Mao had warned his nation against the danger of modern revisionism and foreign subversion. For a nation that had almost nothing to lose economically in opening up to the outside world, such an admonition held no power of deterrence. The establishment especially hated the concept, for the continuing revolution only turned them into prime targets of popular rebellion. In the wake of the Cultural Revolution, there was a well-concerted campaign to restore the collective image of the revolutionary cadres as the "good guys." However, the cadre corps no longer consisted of the legion of youth that had followed Mao from Yanan to Beijing. Now a battered and fast-aging group, officials in both the party and government became prisoners of their past, servants of their relatives' insatiable greed and captives of bribery and flattery. Ideologically, the system was much less zealous and more practical than before the Cultural Revolution, having become acutely aware of the importance of power and self-preservation. That was why it so quietly rallied around Deng Xiaoping when the latter came back to power.

The party's new recruits during and after the Cultural Revolution were, in general, of low quality and ignorant of orthodox Marxism. Many were rebels who were smart enough to compromise with the party machine. They were adept at establishing and using connections. With little sense of moral decency, this group joined the party officials who no longer seemed to care for ideological excellency. Rather, they were great practitioners of nepotism, clientelism, and sycophancy. The extent of corruption in the party was exposed during the rectification campaign in 1985 when thousands of party members were either expelled or "discharged with honor."

The post–Mao Chinese leadership blamed the Cultural Revolution for most of the party's problems and those of Chinese society, for the Cultural Revolution confused people's thinking and destroyed the party's discipline. Some party ideologues waxed nostalgic about the "good old days" before the Cultural Revolution as if the party would have fared much better had the Cultural Revolution not occurred. One thing is certain, however: during the Cultural Revolution, the party apparatus had lost its awesome image. This resulted in a new political equilibrium in Chinese society. In other words, without its charismatic founding father, the post–Mao Chinese government had to move toward what Frederick C. Teiwes called a "legal-rational" government.[43] After the trial of the Cultural Revolution, some of the more insightful Communists arrived at a critical view, not only of the Cultural Revolution, but of some chronic problems within the CCP as a whole. Enlightened party members not only blamed Mao for the disasters of the Cultural Revolution, they also pointed to the lack of a democratic tradition inside the CCP, and even in Chinese culture.[44]

The first couple of years after the Cultural Revolution would see the rise of two kinds of people in the party and government: old cadres, who opposed the Gang of Four, but not necessary Mao, and technocrats, whose expertise was needed by the party for modernization. The intellectuals, who had been so badly persecuted and discredited before and during the Cultural Revolution by the Maoists, proved indispensable in bringing about the post–Mao economic reforms. Here, Deng Xiaoping came back to square one: as had Mao in the 1950s and 1960s, he faced the task of utilizing the talents of the educated elite without allowing them to jeopardize the privilege of the CCP. One way to do this was to give the intellectuals a place in the hall of fame. Intellectuals, the party organs explained, belonged to the working class. Organizational departments of the CCP at all levels and localities went on a drive to recruit members from among the intellectuals. To win them over, the post–Mao Chinese government would also have to acknowledge past errors and redress thousands of cases of persecution. This policy, however, would lead to further questioning of the legitimacy of political campaigns such as the Anti-Rightist Campaign of 1957, in which many Communist officials, including Deng Xiaoping himself, had had a role. Thus, while Deng Xiaoping and reformers in the post–Mao era recognized the need for political decompression, they would find it necessary to keep the lid on the grievances among the intellectuals.

While tens of thousands of intellectuals were absorbed into the ruling party at the expense of its ideological purity, the system continued to produce dissidents.

Given the backlash against the Cultural Revolution, political decompression should not be interpreted as a unilateral policy of the Deng Xiaoping administration, but rather as the party's response to the public repugnance toward left extremism. The party had to change its image from a party of revolutionaries to one of builders and from a party of cadres to one of managers. On the ability to achieve decompression hinged the very survival of the ruling party. It was a policy of necessity, not free choice. Deng Xiaoping knew this, as did his associates such as Zhao Ziyang and Hu Yaobang. Even the hard-liners, such as Deng Liqun and Chun Yun, agreed; they, too, were victims of the Cultural Revolution. The difference would exist in the degrees of decompression, not in the principle. For the reformers, the task was how to introduce a capitalist approach without appearing to betray the revolution. For the hard-liners, the trick was how to protect their vested interests without looking doctrinaire. They would find a common ground in attempts at preserving the party's hegemony in Chinese society.

Needless to say, the devastation of the Cultural Revolution caused unspeakable despair among many Chinese citizens. The gradual thaw after 1976 led to a "mood of introspection and self-doubt."[45] The reaction to years of political totalitarianism and intellectual obscurantism was an increasingly numerous "lost generation" that was ready for an ideological revolt, either direct or indirect, against the CCP. Reminiscences of the Cultural Revolution would turn into a plethora of novels, dramas, and poetry denouncing the past, resulting in a flourishing of literary creativity that China had never seen before, and representing an unprecedented pursuit of new political and philosophical answers to China's problems. This revolt would be as profound as the intellectual ferment of the May 4 era of the 1910s and 1920s. The Communist Party had either to develop a theoretical dimension strong enough to resist the backlash to its misrule before 1976, or it would again be forced to resort to violence to stifle the rebellion.

NOTES

1. Han Zi, *Dadi changshang—Zhongnanhai renwu chenfu neimu* (Inside stories of Zhongnanhai personnel) (Beijing: Zhongguo Dadi Press, 1993), pp. 266–267.

2. Yan Jiaqi and Gao Gao, *Zhongguo wenge shinian shi* (A history of China's ten-year Cultural Revolution) (Beijing: China Studies Press, 1986), pp. 1–44; anonymous, "Peng Zhen zai wenge qianxi" (Peng Zhen on the eve of the Cultural Revolution), *Yin Hai* (Silver Sea), May 1989, pp. 22–43.

3. Hai Rui (1514–1587), a famous official and reformer of the Jiaqing and Longqing periods of the Ming dynasty, was known for his moral courage in fighting bureaucratic corruption.

4. Qi Xin, "Wenge zuoqing de jidu fazhan" (Extreme leftism during the Cultural Revolution), *Qishi Niandai* (Nineteen-Seventies), December 1978, p. 74.

5. Yan and Gao, *History of China's Ten-Year Cultural Revolution*, pp. 102–105.

6. The most outspoken and disturbing summary of the Cultural Revolution is in Wen Yu, Zhongquo zuohuo (*China's Leftist Peril*) (Beijing: Zhaohua Press, 1993).

7. Lin Biao, who was named Mao's successor at the Nineth Congress of the CCP in 1969, died in a plane crash in the Mongolian People's Republic on September 13, 1971, following an abortive coup.

8. Keith Forster, "Factional Politics in Zhejiang, 1973–1976," in A. William Joseph, Christine P. W. Wong, and David Zweig, eds., *New Perspectives on the Cultural Revolution* (Cambridge, Mass.: Harvard University, Council on East Asian Studies, 1991), p. 126

9. Yan and Gao, *History of China's Ten-Year Cultural Revolution*, pp. 337–339.

10. See Institute for the Study of Chinese Communist Problems, *Important CCP Documents of the Great Proletarian Cultural Revolution* (Taipei, Taiwan: Institute for the Study of Chinese Communist Problems, 1973), p. 256.

11. Shu Guang, "Hongshe Jininabei shi yibu xuelei jianzheng" (*The Red Monument* is a witness to blood and tears), *Beijing Spring*, November 1993, p. 88; Zhao Cong, *Wenge yundong licheng shulue* (An outline history of the Cultural Revolution) (Hong Kong: Youlian Research Institute, 1975), 3:410–414.

12. See anonymous, *Hong Sha* (Red shark) (Taibei, Taiwan: Liming Cultural Press, 1993).

13. Dennis Woodward, "Political Power and Gun Barrels: The Role of the PLA," in Bill Brugger and David Kelly eds., *China: The Impact of the Cultural Revolution*, (Stanford, Calif: Stanford University Press, 1990), pp. 71–94.

14. Xiguang Yu, Liangdong Li, and Jianzhong Ni, *Dachao xinqi: Deng Xiaoping nanxun qianqian houhou* (Tidal wave: before and after Deng Xiaoping's tour in south China) (Beijing: Chinese Broadcast and Television Press, 1992), p. 19.

15. Hua Guofeng, "Tuanjie qilai, wei jianshe shehui zhuyi de xiandaihua qiangguo er fendou" (Get united and strive for a modernized socialist country) (Report made at the first meeting of the Fifth People's Congress, on February 26, 1978), *Peking Review*, March 3, 1978, p. 19.

16. Robert M. Field, "The Performance of Industry During the Cultural Revolution: Second Thoughts," *China Quarterly*, 108 (December 1986): 625; see also Robert Field, Kathleen M. McGlynn, and William B. Abnett, "Political Conflict and Industrial Growth in China: 1965–1977," in United States Congress, Joint Economic Committee, *Chinese Economy Post Mao* (Washington, D.C.: U.S. Government Printing Office, 1978), pp. 273–283.

17. David Zweig's characterization of China's countryside during the Cultural Revolution was partial, if not totally wrong. See David Zweig, *Agrarian Radicalism in China, 1968-1981* (Cambridge, Mass.: Harvard University Press, 1989), pp. 62–64, 194.

18. Jonathan D. Spencer, *The Search for Modern China* (W. W. Norton & Co., 1990), p. 606; see also Lucian W. Pye: "Reassessing the Cultural Revolution," *China Quarterly* 108 (December 1986): 1.

19. The image of the urban youth as radicals still committed to Maoist values in the countryside provided by some American scholars is highly questionable. Ideologues were only a small number of the rusticated urban youth and were extremely unpopular among their own group. See Zweig, *Agrarian Radicalism in China*, p. 48.

20. Theoretically, it sounds desirable for a country like China, whose rural areas were backward economically and culturally to transfeer urbanites to rural areas and thus speed the modernization process there. However, as a nation-wide policy enforced by a government lacking in the proper incentive, it was doomed to failure. Any developing country has to find better ways than this to narrow the gap between the city and the village. See Thomas P. Bernstein, *Up to the Mountains and Down to the Villages* (New Haven, Conn.: Yale University Press, 1977), pp. 290–299.

21. Mao Zedong, Speech Delivered at the Second Plenum of the Eighth Congress of the CCP, May 8, 1958; see also Li Min, "Mao Zedong de diwang shixiang" (Mao Zedong's monarchical inclination) *Zhongguo zhi Chun* (China Spring), June 1992, p. 49.

22. Yan and Gao, *History of China's Ten-Year Cultural Revolution*, pp. 71–83; Li Yong et al. eds., *Deaths of famous individuals during the Cultural Revolution*, pp. 113–117, 132–149; 150–154; 181–196; 229–232; 253–278.

23. Peng Deng's conversation with an old friend of Mr. Liang.

24. Brantly Womack, "In Search of Democracy: Public Authority and Popular Power in China," in Brantly Womack ed., *Contemporary Chinese Politics in Historical Perspective* (Cambridge, Mass.: Harvard University Press, 1991), p. 78.

25. Merle Goldman, quoted in L. Pye, "Reassessing the Cultural Revolution," *China Quarterly* 108 (December 1986): 605.

26. Anonymous, "Diyi ci paoda zhang chunqiao" (First bombardment on Zhang Chunqiao), *Shenzhou Shibao* (China Journal), November 19, 1993.

27. Yan and Gao, *History of China's Ten-Year Cultural Revolution*, pp. 261–272.

28. Li et al., eds., *Deaths of Famous Individuals during the Cultural Revolution*, pp. 233–246.

29. Ibid, pp. 327–347; Guo Loji, "Shui zhi zui?" (Whose crime is this?), *Guangming Ribao* (Guangming Daily), June 24, 1979.

30. Lao Gui, *The Bloody Dawn*, also see, "Baoshi huangye de nufan" (Female "criminals" whose bodies were left in the wilderness), *China Spring*, September 1992, pp. 76–81.

31. Zhao, *An Outline History of the Cultural Revolution*, 3: 335–336.

32. Jonathan Unger, "Wither China? Yang Xiguan, Red Capitalists, and the Social Turmoil of the Cultural Revolution," *Modern China* 17 (January 1991): 33; see also 3–37.

33. See Ross Terrill, *China in Our Time: The Epic Saga of the People's Republic from the Communist Victory to Tiananmen Square and Beyond* (New York: Simon and Schuster, 1992), pp. 287–291.

34. Wang Min, "Li Yize gei houlai ren de yidian qishi" (Li Yize's revelation for people after them), *China Spring*, March 1983; p. 26; Gong Xiaoxia, "Bin Bu Gudu de Xianquzhe" (A pioneer whose voice is heard), *China Spring*, December 1988, p. 27.

35. Johnathan Unger, "Wither China," *Modern China* 17 (January 1991): 29.

36. Yan and Gao, *History of China's Ten-Year Cultural Revoltuion*, pp. 557–559, 613–621; Commentator, "Weida de siwu yundong" (The great April 5th movement), *Zhongguo Qingnian Bao* (Chinese Youth Daily), November 12, 1978.

37. Anonymous, "To a Great Woman," David S. G. Goodman, ed., *Beijing Street Voices*, p. 32; also Yong Yu, "Animal Crackers," in ibid., pp. 21–25; anonymous, "Paean to Qing Ming," in ibid., p. 39.

38. Deng was appointed vice-premier on the recommendation of Zhou Enlai in 1975.

39. Some scholars challenged such definition, arguing that the Cultural Revolution had come to an end in 1970. The thesis of the ten-year turmoil was coined by the restored political establishment.

40. Womack, "In Search of Democracy," p. 78.

41. Central Committee of the Chinese Communist Party, "Guanyu jianguo yilai ruogan lishi wenti de jueyi" (Resolution on certain historical issues since the founding of the People's Republic of China) (Beijing: People's Press, 1981), pp. 24–25; *People's Daily*, July 1, 1981; see also Hu Yaobang's speech quoted in Immanuel C. Y. Hsu, *The Rise of Modern China* (New York: Oxford University Press, 1983), pp. 827–828.

42. Deng said in 1978: "So far as a cat catches mice, it is a good cat no matter whether it is white or black."

43. Frederick C. Teiwes, *Leadership, Legitimacy, and Conflict in China* (Armonk, N.Y.: M. E. Sharpe, 1983), p. 8.

44. Zhou Yang, "Sanci weida de sixiang jiefang yundong" (Three great thought-emancipation campaigns), *People's Daily*, May 7, 1979, Sun Ruiyi and Li Yanqi, "Shehui zhuyi guojia buneng gao 'sixiang fan,'" (In a socialist state there should not be "thought criminals"), *Beijing Daily*, August 4, 1979; Commentator, "Fengjian zhuyi sixiang yidu yinggai shuqing" (Wipe out the remnants of feudal thinking), *People's Daily*, July 18, 1979.

45. Fox Butterfield, *China: Alive in the Bitter Sea* (New York: New York Times Books, 1982), p. 447.

3

A Transition in the Making: Reform and Its Consequences

This chapter describes the political and economic reforms in China after the Cultural Revolution as the catalyst of sociopolitical transition. We shall first briefly discuss the immediate sociopolitical conditions prior to the reforms. Second, we will depict the reforms themselves by analyzing their major policy components. Finally, we shall discuss the immediate, ongoing impact of the reforms on China's sociopolitical foundations.

THE IMMEDIATE SOCIOPOLITICAL CONDITIONS OF THE REFORMS

The Cultural Revolution left the PRC with disastrous sociopolitical legacies: hundreds of thousands of people from almost all social strata had been persecuted mentally and physically, and the national economy was on the brink of bankruptcy. As a result, most people, including many government officials and party members, had lost their faith in the party and the official ideology—Mao Zedong Thought. The people's changing attitudes toward the party and its ideology have since then been expressed through continuous and spontaneous mass demonstrations, public speeches by activists, and in the popular arts and private correspondence.

The most notable of the mass demonstrations was the 1976 Tiananmen incident (*Tiananmen Shijian*), when thousands of citizens from a variety of social classes and occupations marched to Tiananmen Square carrying wreaths to memorialize Zhou Enlai, who had died in January of the same year and was esteemed for his compassion for the masses and for his role in checking the "ultra-leftists," such as the Gang of Four, within the party. People read poems and made speeches expressing their displeasure with the Gang of Four, which was nonetheless in power. They also implicitly expressed their grievances against the then paramount leader, Chairman Mao, because he was believed to have been corrupted and blinded by the Gang of Four, and hence, to be encouraging the latter's tyranny. Although the demonstration was suppressed by the Gang of Four, spiritual solidarity among the people, especially the younger generation, which had been disillusioned by the turmoil of the Cultural Revolution, was reinforced through this mass demonstration. Their common grievances against the tyranny and their suspicions about the "Great Leader" and the "Great, Glorious and Correct Party" were given full publicity.[1]

Only two years after the 1976 Tiananmen incident, in the fall of 1978 and the spring of 1979, Beijing citizens, led by worker and student activists, began to write big-character posters on a wall near Xidan Avenue in Beijing, demanding democratic reforms. The wall later came to be called the "Xidan Democracy Wall." The posters on the Democracy Wall drew great public attention and enthusiasm, even from quite a number of foreign observers. Several quite intriguing ideas were advocated in this movement: eliminating one-party totalitarian rule, establishing multiparty and bicameral parliamentary democracy, calling for the general election of a national leader, and reevaluating Mao Zedong Thought (then the official ideology) as well as Mao himself.

On November 15, 1978, for instance, Wei Jingshen, who was one of the most articulate advocates of civil liberty and democracy, posted one of the most well-known posters of the Democracy Wall Movement. In this poster, entitled the "Fifth Modernization: Democracy and Etc.," Wei called for a restructuring of China's political system. He argued that the foremost task for the Chinese people was to "get back what inherently belongs to them"—the right to select their own representatives to serve the people's interests.[2] Moreover, he pointed out that the totalitarian political system, especially under Mao, was the root of all China's sociopolitical disasters, such as the Great Leap Forward, the Anti-Rightist Campaign, and the Cultural Revolution. He believed, therefore, that unless there was a "fifth modernization"—democratization [added to the modernization agenda], the other four modernizations would be only lip service, since political freedom was the foremost prerequisite of any social progress.[3] In late 1979, Wei was arrested and sentenced for supplying "national secrets" to Western reporters and encouraging the overthrow of the socialist system.

The idea of a multiparty system was also suggested by Fu Shenqi, an editor of the liberal underground journal, *Responsibility*. In an article entitled, "Democracy and Socialism," he argued that in a "socialist" country such as China, different parties can serve to represent diverse policy viewpoints and strategies, all of which serve the common interests of the working class. "Independent, autonomous political parties," he suggested, "are of decisive significance for democracy. Where there are not two or more such independent parties, democracy cannot fully develop. In such places the legislature always becomes a cover for one-party dictatorship and the press becomes an echo of the single party."[4]

In early 1979, activists of the Democracy Wall Movement formed political-cultural associations such as the Thaw Society, Enlightenment Society, and China Human Rights Alliance in an attempt to spread the ideas of political reform. In addition to organizing symposia, these associations published their own journals, such as *Beijing Spring (Beijing zhi chun)*, *April Fifth Forum (Siwu luntan)*, and *Exploration (Tansuo)*, which were widely circulated among the youth and the educated in many major cities. These journals discussed a wide range of topics related to almost all kinds of sociopolitical issues: from freedom of speech, freedom of assembly, universal suffrage, human rights, antifeudalism, and the reevaluation of Mao Zedong Thought to the multiparty system. If the 1976 Tiananmen incident witnessed people's suspicions against the correctness of the party and its leader, the 1978–1979 Democracy Wall Movement in Beijing further incited the people to rethink the legitimacy of party's rule and the correctness of the official ideology.

By the mid-1980s, several nationally renowned intellectuals joined the public to demand deeper sociopolitical reform and more political freedom. In 1986, Fang Lizhi, a worldwide noted astrophysicist, made a series of influential speeches at several China's major universities. Known as the "Chinese Sakharov," Fang in his speeches vigorously advocated such Western liberal ideas as free elections, free speech, a free press, multiparty competition, and the rule of law. He argued that the totalitarian one-party rule in China was based on military conquest, not merit, and that its overall record in the past thirty-five years could only be considered a failure. Furthermore, Fang urged the students to fight for their rights.[5]

Liu Binyan of *Xinhua News Agency*, one of China's most preeminent investigative reporters, suggested that the Chinese people should abandon any illusions about the merits of the party and its official ideology. Liu, who had been persecuted in the 1957 Anti-Rightist Campaign for his criticism of the party's bureaucratism, summoned the people to unchain themselves from four fantasies:

(1) that socialism is perfect; (2) that the Communist party is infallible; (3) that Marxism-Leninism is eternal truth; and (4) that there is a deep chasm between socialism and capitalism and that nothing in the capitalist societies that took place in the past several hundred years should be given proper recognition.[6]

The people's grievances were also reflected in the cultural realm. Using art to express grievances against tyranny has long been a Chinese tradition, which can be traced back at least to Lu Xun's satirical essays against the then Guomindang rule in mainland China. Without exception, once again the arts were utilized by the people to express their dissenting sentiment against Communist totalitarian rule following the death of Mao. Beginning with so-called the "Literature of Wounds" (named after a short story, "The Wound," by Lu Xinhua, which was published in August 1978), fiction, drama, journalism, poetry, songs, the fine arts, and film all began to vividly present the people's sufferings in a series of political campaigns under the totalitarian rule of the CCP. A typical example of the Literature of Wounds was a film, *Legend of Tianyun Mountain* (1982), which explicitly implied that people's sufferings—from the Great Leap Forward, the Anti-Rightist Campaign, and the Cultural Revolution—all resulted from the party's arbitrary policies and rigid ideology. After the film was released, it became a hot topic among the people, who vigorously sought an analogy between the story told in the film and the reality of their daily life.

Treading in the steps of the Literature of Wounds, some people began to further explore alternative solutions for their perceived political depression. In the summer of 1988, a six-part television documentary, *"River Elegy"* (*He Shang*) was aired. Written by Su Xiaokang and Wang Luxiang with counsel from the economist Li Yining and the scientist Jin Guantao, its script singled out the Yellow River, the dragon, and the Great Wall as symbols of the Chinese nation's acceptance of long-standing totalitarian rule, fanaticism to official dogma, and ignorance of the outside. More significant, in its conclusion the film called for national liberation from the culturally rooted totalitarian tradition and urged a new national orientation—"to the blue sea," which symbolized "openness" and "freedom." It implied that instead of *waiting for* a "wise and just emperor" as they had done for centuries, the people should control their own destinies by abandoning all "spiritual shackles" (such as Confucianism and Maoism) and choosing a more open society.[7]

All these incidents constitute sociopolitical preconditions for Deng Xiaoping's reforms, which that ultimately transformed the Chinese polity from a totalitarian to an authoritarian regime. In response to the people's discontent and the devastating consequences of the Cultural Revolution, the top party leaders, especially Deng Xiaoping, who had personally suffered the most visible political persecution in this upheaval, realized the urgent need to reform the party, the state system, and the economy. These reforms, as Deng defined in his important speech at the Third Plenum of the Eleventh Congress of the CCP, "concerned the life and death of the party and country."[8] "Without reforms," Deng claimed, "the entire cause of socialism in China would be ruined."[9] In private, Deng also repeatedly talked to his close associates such as Ye Jianying, Chen Yun, and Wang Zhen about the necessity and urgency of the reforms. After experiencing a series of "ultra-left" political campaigns—especially the Cultural Revolution—which had taken a heavy toll on the party's reputation and the people's belief in the official ideology, these surviving leaders sensed that they had to set new national goals in order to rekindle the masses' belief in the Communist regime.

To these leaders, the reform was also a last chance to revive their personal careers, which had boomed through the long-time armed struggle with warlords, the Japanese troops, and the Guomindang, culminating in the 1949 Communist victory, but had then been shattered during the Cultural Revolution. They had invested most of their lives in the "course of Chinese revolution," which marked their personal careers and influenced their success. After the death of Mao which, in a sense, unleashed this group of pragmatic leaders, the reform could be seen as another opportunity to conclude their careers on a glorious note.

In short, because of the sociopolitical conditions after the Cultural Revolution, reform became socially desirable for the people, who sought a better life, and politically necessary and acceptable for the leaders, who wanted to maintain their ruling position. The reform, therefore, was expected to give the people a better life—with economic well-being and some degree of political relaxation—and also to consolidate the ruling position of the new leaders. In the minds of the leadership, these two objectives were interrelated: economic betterment and relative political relaxation in the society could generate popular support for the new leadership.

AN OVERVIEW OF DENG'S EARLY REFORM PROGRAMS

This sociopolitical transition started in late 1978, when the Third Plenum of the Eleventh Central Committee of the Chinese Communist Party was held to set a new direction of political and economic development in this country. The plenum, as Tang Tsou put it, was "the landmark of the beginning of a new historic era in China."[10] It had at least two significant impacts on the sociopolitical development of contemporary China after 1949. First, it officially put an end to large-scale political mass movements, such as the Cultural

Revolution, and declared the beginning of a series of unprecedented political and economic reforms which later shook the entire society.[11] Deng Xiaoping and his supporters even proudly declared this meeting to be the outset of a "second revolution," a successor to the first Communist revolution of 1921–1949.[12]

Second, the plenum paved the way for a group of more pragmatic (or less dogmatic) party leaders to regain dominant political power. The greatest beneficiary was Deng Xiaoping himself, who later came to be "the chief architect" for the reforms.[13] Some China scholars even claimed that the meeting was just as important as the Zunyi Conference of January 1935, which established Mao Zedong's leadership in the CCP by making him the head of a three-man group in charge of military affairs.[14] In short, the Third Plenum signified the beginning of a significant sociopolitical change which was conditioned by the people's discontent with current party-state policies and their doubt about the official ideology. Moreover, this change eventually led to a political transition from one type of regime to another.

Generally speaking, the reform agenda designed by the new leadership consisted of two major elements—political reforms and economic reforms. The political reforms fell into two major categories: first, reassessing the previous official ideology—Mao Zedong Thought—and searching for new ideological principles; and second, redefining the role of the Chinese Communist Party and the relationship between the party and the state in the course of the Socialist Four Modernizations. The economic reforms were conducted in three areas: in the production system, the market system, and the income distribution system. While in reality, the political and economic reforms were interrelated or mutually inclusive, for the purpose of analysis we shall look at each reform separately.

At the beginning of the reform, the first and most serious challenge that Deng and his associates faced was the previous ideological dogma—Mao Zedong Thought. Orthodox Maoists such as Hua Guofeng and Wang Dongxing, who had been hand-picked by Mao and then remained in power after Mao's death, continued to adhere to Mao's thought and would block any new policies that contradicted whatever Mao had said.

On February 7, 1977, Hua Guofeng, the new chairman of the CCP, announced the doctrine of "two whatevers" (*Liangge Fanshi*). "We will," he asserted, "resolutely support whatever decisions Chairman Mao made; we will unflinchingly obey whatever instructions Chairman Mao issued."[15] Identified completely with Mao's ideology and policies, the doctrine not only posed obstacles to any possible reforms, it also prohibited Deng Xiaoping and his associates from coming to power, since Mao in 1976 had said that Deng Xiaoping should not be given any significant power because of his negligence of class struggle and his alleged involvement in the April protest of that year. To Deng and his associates, therefore, Maoism, and especially an ossified interpretation of it, became a great spiritual and psychological obstacle, both within the party and among the people, to the exploration of any innovative policies or the acceptance of new leadership. As Deng put it in early December 1978: "If a party, a country, or a nation approaches everything dogmatically, applies rigid thought, and is superstitious, then its vitality will stop. The party and state will collapse."[16] Publicly reassessing, if not repudiating, the previous official ideology of Mao's Thought thus became vital for Deng and his associates in order to win public support for the new leadership and remove political obstacles to the much-needed reforms.

Deng and his supporters carefully started their reassessment of the official ideology from an epistemological standpoint. They first attempted to tell the party and the people how to judge the truth of ideology. In May 1978, several months before the Third Plenum, *Guangming Ribao*, an official organ which was well known for its liberal perspectives and close political association with the pragmatic leaders, published an article entitled "Practice Is the Sole Criterion for Testing Truth." This article explicitly suggested that instead of the words of the "saints" (namely, Marx, Lenin, and Mao), only practice should be the criterion for judging ideas, laws, or ideologies.[17] Furthermore, the article boldly urged the party and the people to dispense with the outmoded way of thinking and to blaze a new trail for China's sociopolitical progress. The publication of the article met with widespread enthusiasm among the people and within the party, as the entire country was desperately searching for a way out of the shadow of the Cultural Revolution. A nationwide discussion followed the article, having been (either explicitly or implicitly) orchestrated by the pragmatic leaders, particularly Deng Xiaoping and Hu Yaobang. In June, Deng Xiaoping drove the momentum further by making an important speech at the Military Political Work Conference that called on everyone "to use the method of seeking truth from facts, proceeding from reality and integrating theory with practice."[18] He also argued that the basic tenet of Mao Zedong Thought was respect for the facts.[19] Respect for facts then became the substitute for the worship of any ideological dogma or charismatic leader.

After the attempt to whip up consensus on this epistemological issue among the populace and the party members, Deng and his supporters further consolidated and legitimized their victory in the Third Plenum in December 1978. In this historic meeting, they affirmed the principle that practice was the only correct criterion to evaluate truth and asserted that in order to achieve the Four Modernizations, it was necessary to "emancipate the thinking of the party, to study new circumstances, things, and questions, and to uphold the principle of seeking truth from facts."[20] To further shatter the basis of the "two whatevers" doctrine upheld by the Maoist standpatters, Deng and his supporters boldly pointed out that Mao was no saint, and therefore, what he said and did was not necessarily correct: "It would not be Marxist to demand that a revolutionary leader be free of all shortcomings and errors."[21] This was only the beginning of a reassessment and a partial repudiation of the previous official ideology—Mao Zedong Thought and Mao himself.

This process of the reassessment of Mao and the repudiation of his thought finally culminated in the Sixth Plenum of the CCP Central Committee, which adopted a "Resolution on Certain Questions in the History of Our Party since the Founding of the People's Republic of China." This historic document, which was initiated by the pragmatic leaders under Deng, systematically and "objectively" reassessed the role of Mao as a party-state leader and that of Mao's thought as the official ideology. While reaffirming Mao's contribution to the Chinese Communist movement, the document noted that Mao personally was responsible for a series of "ultra-left" and "excessive" political campaigns, including the Anti-Rightist Movement of 1957, the Great Leap Forward of 1958–1959, and, especially, the Cultural Revolution of 1966–1976, which almost cost the country its well-being. As Deng once "objectively" put it, as a revolutionary leader, Mao was "seventy percent correct and thirty percent wrong."[22] In short, the new leaders deidolized Mao by convincing the people that, as a human being, he had made mistakes and been limited by his secular vision.

The deidolization of Mao as a revolutionary leader then logically led to detheologization of Mao's thought. Since Mao as a leader was not perfect, his thought was far from flawless. The Resolution declared that while Mao Zedong Thought had made significant contributions to the Chinese Communist revolution, especially during the armed struggle against the Guomindang regime and the War of Resistance against Japan, it had serious flaws, in terms of its ability to build a new people's republic after 1949. Particularly, Mao's "ultra-left" ideas of class struggle in a socialist society and "continued revolution under the proletariat dictatorship" were erroneous, because these concepts had been the ideological basis for a series of political upheavals, such as the Anti-Rightist Campaign and the Cultural Revolution.[23] Mao's insistence on the continued revolution and class struggle, Deng pointed out, was based on a "faulty judgment of the Chinese reality."[24] For example, in reference to the Cultural Revolution, which was initiated based on the "theory of continued revolution under the proletariat dictatorship," the Dengists asserted that this upheaval was "divorced both from the party organization and from the masses."[25] The party assessment concluded that the Cultural Revolution was initiated by one leader, Mao, who had labored under "misapprehension" and had been taken advantage of by radicals with the ideological support of the theory of "continued revolution." The final result of the Cultural Revolution was "catastrophe to the party, the state and the whole people."[26] In fact, the assessment of the Cultural Revolution had a double-edged impact on Chinese politics in the post–Cultural Revolution era. First, the repudiation of the Cultural Revolution seemed to be at the time one of the most expedient measures to win popular support for the new leadership, since this sociopolitical upheaval had been a nightmare for almost every Chinese citizen. Second, the repudiation of the Cultural Revolution was also a very effective way to prove that Mao and his thought were far from perfect, because this sociopolitical catastrophe was the most visible evidence of his mistakes. In short, according to the new leaders, a major part of Mao's thought was no longer applicable to the reality of post-1949 China. By criticizing (or "reassessing") Mao's thought, Deng and his associates paved the way for their political innovations—the post–Mao political and economic reforms.

It is also worth noting that this was the first time in the history of the CCP since 1935 and of the PRC that the party had publicly criticized Mao and his thought. Mao had become the undisputed leader of the CCP in the party's 1935 Zunyi Conference. Mao Zedong Thought was officially adopted as the ideological "guiding principle," along with the theories of Marxism-Leninism, for the CCP at the party's Seventh National Congress in 1945. Since 1949, when Mao became the paramount leader and his thought the official ideology for the entire nation, neither Chairman Mao nor Mao Zedong Thought had been challenged, or even seriously questioned by the party or the people in a public or "objective" manner.[27] Therefore, it was inevitable that the assessment of Mao and his thought would bring about significant sociopolitical consequences in contemporary China, thus catalyzing a political transition.

In a speech entitled "Reforming the Leadership Institutions of the Party and the State" and given at an enlarged meeting of the Politburo on August 18, 1980,[28] Deng for the first time put forth the agenda of "political restructuring" in terms of the role of the party and the relationship between party and state.[29] In this speech, he pointed out that the overconcentration of power in the central party and government organs, or, worse, in a single individual, had been the source of numerous political turmoils, especially the Cultural Revolution. This overconcentration of power had been incarnated specifically in the form of the "party's monistic leadership [dang de yiyuanhua lingdao]" which had evolved into the "replacement of the government by the party [yidang daizheng]." As Deng put it, "The monistic leadership of the party frequently becomes leadership by a single individual."[30] The overconcentration of power, Deng continued, "hinders the exercises of the socialist democratic system and democratic centralism within the party; hampers the socialist construction;

depresses the collective wisdom; [and] leads to arbitrary decisions by the individual."[31]

To solve this problem, Deng proposed to prohibit party leaders at all levels from concurrently holding executive positions, and to separate the party from the state in terms of their functions and institutions.[32] As a result, in 1980 the then party chairman, Hua Guofeng, resigned from his premiership, while Deng and five other party leaders resigned from their positions as vice-premiers. In addition, many first secretaries of the party at various levels relinquished their concurrently held positions as chief executive officers.

With regard to the separation of the party and the government, Deng specifically suggested that the State Council and local governments at all levels should discuss, make decisions on, and send out documents pertaining to administrative affairs, while the party apparatus at all levels should cease to interfere in the administrative affairs. He also proposed to change the system of giving responsibility to the administrator or manager of the grass-roots unit (*jiceng danwei*), under the leadership of the unit's party committee. Instead, responsibility would be given to the administrator or manager under the leadership and supervision of the unit's management committee, the board of trustees, or the joint committee of unified economic units.

In 1987, the Thirteenth Party Congress further institutionalized Deng's ideas on redefining of the relationship between the party and the state and the party's role. In this meeting, seven major measures were adopted to reform the party and government leadership systems.[33] The seven measures were the separation of party and government functions, delegation of powers to lower levels, establishment of a public service system, regular dialogue between the people and the party, perfection of the socialist democracy, and strengthening of the socialist legal system. Of these measures, the separation of party and government functions and the delegation of powers to the lower levels seemed most substantial.

Following Deng's suggestions, the Thirteenth Party Congress defined the function of the government as dealing with daily administrative and managerial activities and possessing autonomy in making its own decisions, while the role of the party was to exercise ideological and moral leadership by organizing and summoning its membership in achieving the national goal—the Four Modernizations. It seemed that the government function was defined more concretely than the role of the party. The government business seemed concrete and inevitably tangible, and its decisions and activities were related to the people's everyday life, including their economic and financial problems. However, the party's ideological and moral leadership, which lacked the power to interfere in tangible activities, seemed intangible and quite ambiguous. In reality, party leaders without concurrent positions in the government could hardly exercise "leadership."[34] The ambiguity in the definition of party's new "leadership" and the inability of party leaders to function effectively seemed to be a direct result of Deng's political reform initiatives, which found ready acceptance by millions of Chinese people weary of party control. Moreover, all these initiatives greatly contributed to a fundamental change in the role of the party in Chinese sociopolitical life.

Along with the political reform, an economic reform was initiated at the end of the 1970s by the new leadership. In time, the economic reform, which brought about economic growth, became the cornerstone of the post-Mao Communist rule in China, with Deng Xiaoping named as the "chief architect" of this economic restructuring. Generally speaking, the economic reform had two interrelated goals: to improve the living standards of the people and the material wealth of the society; and second, through the improvement in the economic well-being of the entire society, to reestablish the party's popular image, which had been severely shattered during the Cultural Revolution, and hence to reinforce the ruling position of the party's new leadership. As Deng himself put it early in 1979, "If the social productive forces are not developed and people's material life is not improved, then our *socialist political system* cannot be consolidated."[35] For Deng and his supporters, the economic reform can also be seen as a *means*, or a set of tools, to be used in the service of the fundamental political *end*: a revitalization of the party's popularity and the restoration of its legitimacy. Therefore, the original intention of the economic reform was by no means to establish a "capitalistic" economic system under a Communist rule.

The economic reform was first introduced in rural areas in the late 1970s and later extended to urban locales in the early 1980s. It has been carried out in three major economic areas: the production system, the marketplace, and the income distribution system.

The reform in the production and distribution systems was first attempted in the form of the "production responsibility system" (*shengchan zeren zhi*) in rural areas. This was, in essence, an incentive system granting responsibilities to peasants for their production and distributing income according to their fulfillment of the responsibilities.

In 1978, at the Third Plenum of the Eleventh Central Committee, the party, under the leadership of Deng Xiaoping, made a resolution on agricultural reform. In some sense, the resolution actually served as the official endorsement for the earlier experiments of rural reform in some provinces, such as Sichuan under Zhao Ziyang, who was the then party chief of that province. Specifically, this resolution urged that remuneration for work should be based on the principle of "to each according to his work." It also directed that private plots and sideline production were now "necessary adjuncts of the

socialist economy and must not be interfered with."[36] Later, in 1980, the
Central Committee Document number 75 specified the methods to implement
the "production responsibility system."[37] One method was "to assign each
household an output quota" (*Baochan daohu*). According to this method, a
township should allot land to each household; in the township, a production
team and each household then signed a contract on the output quota that the
household should be obligated to fulfill and the income it could consequently
make.

Another typical method of rural responsibility system was "to give full
production responsibility to each household" (*Baogan daohu*). Under this
method, the household signed a contract with the village authority to assume all
responsibility for production on the allotted land and to bear the entire
responsibility for its own profit or loss. While this method seemed more risky,
it could be more rewarding to households that worked hard and experienced
good luck.

By the early 1980s, the rural production responsibility system had been
implemented in all the provinces. According to an official report in 1980, 90
percent of the villages in the townships had adopted some form of the
responsibility system.[38] The positive results of the production and distribution
reform, as James Wang summarized, were encouragement for the peasants to
work harder in order to receive more income. The system allowed the peasants
to manage their own production under the most favorable conditions rather
than under the arbitrary (or bureaucratic) official instructions, thereby granting
the peasants more autonomy and avoiding the problem of constant complaints
by peasants about the unfair distribution of income.[39] This reform consequently
brought about a high growth rate in agricultural production. During
1981–1985, the average annual growth rate of agricultural output was 10
percent, as compared to 3 percent before the reform.[40]

Following the reform in the rural production and distribution system, in
1984, Deng Xiaoping, with his then chief assistant Zhao Ziyang, initiated a
similar reform for the urban (or industrial) areas. The guiding principle of the
reform in urban production and distribution, Deng instructed, was "to introduce
the Responsibility System," which had been proved successful in rural areas.[41]
In addition, he further added that this reform was also "to delegate real power
to the persons who take the responsibility for production."[42]

According to a document entitled "Regulations on Further Extension of
Autonomy of State-Owned Enterprises," which was issued in 1984 by the State
Council, a state-owned "production unit" (*shengchan danwei*) could sign a
contract with the state obligating the unit to submit to the state a certain
amount of taxes and profits and allowing it to retain for its use any, or almost
any, amount above the set quota.[43] This was called the "contract responsibility

system" (*chengbao jingying zhi*). Under this system, the ownership of the production unit was separated from the its operational functions. A production unit was "truly made a relatively independent economic entity." This meant that such units must operate and manage their own affairs, assume responsibility for their own profits and losses, and develop themselves as "legal persons with certain rights and duties."[44] The document, which was crafted under the instruction of Deng and Zhao, also urged production unit managers to assume "full responsibility" and the party leaders in the units to "provide active support," rather than leadership, to the managers, with the purpose of establishing a unified direction in production and operation.[45] This also meant that production unit managers must have the power to determine matters such as work assignments and decide wages and bonuses, while they must also be responsible for profits and losses. Under this reform, a successful production unit could retain any profit above the quota set by the state. The manager of the unit had the power to determine how to dispose of the retained profit, such as by rewarding hard-working and skillful workers or improving worker housing. By the end of 1987, 82 percent of the medium and large state-owned production units had adopted the contract responsibility system.[46]

In 1986, the State Council issued a decree urging small-sized production units to adopt the "leasing management system" (*zulin jingying zhi*) and medium and large units to explore a "joint stock system" (*gufen zhi*).[47] The leasing management system called for all small-sized state-owned enterprises with fixed assets of less than 1.5 million yuan (about $400,000)—mostly retail service, repair, and catering businesses—to be leased out under contract to individuals or cooperatives for a period of five years. The leasing contract should be bid in public. The individual or cooperative who won the bid could manage the unit independently, without government supervision, provided that rents and taxes were paid to the state.

Under the joint stock system, medium and large state-owned enterprises could voluntarily become joint stock companies with limited liability.[48] New companies thus became shareholding enterprises with stocks purchased by workers of and individuals outside the enterprises. Members of the boards of directors could be either shareholding or non-shareholding; the latter were elected by the workers and small individual shareholders to represent their interests.

Under the new production and distribution systems, the most qualified directors for the production units were selected on a competitive basis through public biding. Most old-time party cadres were undoubtedly left out because of their incompetence in production management. The new leaders might still be members of the party, or if they were not, local party cells would eagerly enroll them. In either case, the new leaders (or directors) would be more receptive to nontraditional management techniques and much less concerned with ideological correctness.

The economic reform in the production and income distribution arenas in both rural and urban areas eventually had a striking political impact on the party's leadership and organizations, especially those at the grass-roots level. Under this shakeup of the economic structure, it was doubtful that local party organizations could continue to function in the same ways as before the reform. It was even more questionable whether they could continue to play the "vanguard" role to *lead* and *control* the masses in each production unit in the course of this unprecedented social change.

Along with the reforms in the production and distribution system in rural and urban areas, a reform in the marketplace was launched almost simultaneously. It was designed to give the reins to a more market-oriented economy which seemed, the new leadership, the most attractive way to get out of the post–Cultural Revolution economic stagnation. The guiding principle of market reform was first made by the new leadership at the Third Plenum of the Eleventh Central Committee, late in 1978. While the principle seemed to be only subtly defined at the meeting, it was discernible in its fundamental intention, which was to depart decisively from the old government-controlled market. The communiqué issued by the plenum urged the party and the government to comply with the "law of value" (which denotes the equilibrium of supply and demand, as a natural law) in developing the nation's economy. Economic planners could follow the law of value by monitoring the market. The market, of course, should not be totally controlled by the government. In short, the meeting called for the "use of market mechanisms to supplement the state plan." This decision can also be as seen the first green light for a government relaxation on prices of some retail commodities.

Despite some early scattered experiments after the 1978 plenum, the market reform, especially price relaxation, was not really advanced in an energetic way until late 1984, when the party issued a major document on urban reform at the Third Plenum of the Twelfth Party Congress. The document, entitled the "Decisions on the Reform of Economic Structure," first defined "the use of the market mechanism as one of the inherent attributes of the socialist economic system."[49] The political meaning of this definition was that since the use of market mechanism is "socialist" in nature, economic planners should not see market and price relaxation as a political taboo—as they had done over the past several decades. Deng Xiaoping went so far as to assure the people that the use of the market mechanism was politically and ideologically correct. He said:

Whether more use of the market mechanism or government plan is not the vital distinction between socialism and capitalism. Planned economy is not equivalent of socialism, while capitalism also has a plan; market economy is not the equivalent of capitalism, while socialism also has a market. The government plan and the use of the market mechanism are only economic means.[50]

What Deng meant is that the market mechanism could be seen as an apolitical or neutral means to achieve economic prosperity within the ideological domain of socialism, so that leaders and the masses should not be afraid that they will make any political mistakes when utilizing the market mechanism, such as relaxing price controls to encourage free competition.

Under this party directive concerning market reform, the state had, since 1984, gradually relaxed price controls on certain retail commodities. First, the central government readjusted "irrational" prices on some commodities (prices set according to political objectives and arbitrary considerations), such as by reducing the prices on farm tools and increasing the prices on food products to encourage peasants to produce more.[51] Second, the government gradually lifted price controls over most food and light industrial products, whose prices had been tightly controlled by the state for several decades through an elaborate rationing system in the form of nearly 100 kinds of government-issued coupons. Such coupons, for meat, food oil, grain products, cloth, bikes, sewing machines, and so on, were gradually abandoned.[52] By 1988, prices on over 50 percent of all retail commodities—including food products and household electronic appliances—had been solely determined by the "market mechanism," the equilibrium of supply and demand. The prices on most of the remaining commodities had been only partially controlled through price ceilings set by the government.[53]

By 1988 capital goods were also being distributed, to a large degree, through market and other noncentral planning channels. In the same year, 71 percent of the means of production supplied to the state-owned enterprises were obtained through the market or other means outside the state distribution system.[54] Most of the remaining goods were controlled under a dual-price system: any goods allocated through central planning channels (including steel, coal, oil, cotton, and automobiles) would still carry state-set prices. However, goods sold outside those channels would be priced so as to bring supply and demand into equilibrium. The state would have little or no direct involvement in this second market, and hence, price changes would occur automatically.

As a result of the market reform, the linkage between production and consumption was reestablished through the use of the market mechanism. Motivated by the opportunity to make more profit or avoid losing money, producers began to take the market's temperature and then make their decision on the types and quantity of production accordingly. As producers now were anxious to meet various demands in the market, consumers should have found more choices of products at reasonable prices. Unfortunately, this was not the case for the first several years of market reform because "freer prices under conditions of excess demand, as is generally the case in socialist economies, often led to sharp price increases, thereby contributing to inflation."[55] Urban households immediately experienced the effect of price decontrol: food prices had risen by 37 percent by 1985, while by 1989, they had increased by as much as 250 percent over the 1985 base. In 1989, the actual overall inflation rate was at least 20 percent for retail goods in urban areas.[56]

The dual-price system also contributed in a major way to another increasingly serious problem—growing corruption among government officials. When goods were sold at two different prices and one much higher than the other, there is a large potential profit for those who have access to goods allocated at low state-set prices, which they can sell at high market prices. The dual-price system actually provided opportunities for the government officials, who happened to have power to control the goods allocated through central planning channels, to conduct "official profiteering" (*Guandao*). These officials, and even their children, diverted low-priced goods away from priority sectors and then reaped large profits by selling them to whoever would pay the going price. By the late 1980s, "official profiteering" had become rampant, although data were not publicly available that would allow one to measure its extent. Complaints about official profiteering could be heard from a wide range of the populace.

THE IMPACTS OF THE REFORM ON PARTY LEADERSHIP AND THE OFFICIAL IDEOLOGY

Party organizations and the official ideology, were the two mighty pillars sustaining the Communist totalitarian rule in China. The economic and political reform, which was based on the somewhat expedient considerations of improving the party's image and maintaining its ruling position following the Cultural Revolution, actually brought about significant counteractive side-effects on the party's organization and the official ideology. While the economic reform boosted the average growth rate of China's gross national product (GNP) up to 9 percent during 1978–1990, it by no means salvaged the party's image.[57] Although the political reform gave people more freedom to explore and practice new ideas, it neither heightened party morale nor established a guiding ideological principle for society.

As the economic reform and restructuring proceeded rather swiftly in both rural and urban areas, the party organization seemed to become more obsolete in terms of its role in this fundamental sociopolitical change. Thus, a continuous redefinition of the role, if not the nature, of the ruling party became an urgent, yet difficult, task for the post–Mao leadership. In his directives for political reform, issued in 1980 and 1987, Deng Xiaoping defined the party's role in the reform and its relationship with the state apparatus.[58] According to Deng's definition, the party and the state should be separated from each other in terms of their functions and institutions. The government should deal with *tangible* administrative and managerial activities and have the autonomy make its own decisions, while the party should exercise only *intangible*, ideological and moral leadership by calling on its members to achieve national economic prosperity. In terms of an institutional separation of the party and the government, Deng further prohibited party leaders at all levels from concurrently holding executive positions.[59] According to this mandate, many party secretaries at various levels had to relinquish their concurrently held positions as chief executive officers. The implementation of such policies stripped party leaders and organizations, especially at the local and grass-roots levels, of their "real power" (*shiquan*) to direct administrative and managerial affairs, and hence, of their control over the masses.

In the process of the rural economic reform, the implementation of the responsibility system, under which individual households could contract for land and manage production independently, deprived rural party leaders of their power to control the production and lives of the peasants. As the rural party leaders' managerial and supervisory powers drastically diminished, their income also declined. The local media reported many instances of rural party leaders abandoning their party posts and converting themselves into regular farmers in order to make a better life out of the reform. Unlike their fellow farmers, these former officials could use their "connections" to obtain what they needed.[60] In short, the party apparatus in rural areas no longer functioned as the "leading core" (*lingdao hexin*). Instead, it existed in name only.

Similarly, in the process of the urban economic reform, the party organizations also lost their cohesiveness and leading role in many production and service units. A 1984 party document on urban reform required the party secretaries of each production and service unit to turn over managerial authority to the unit managers.[61] It also transferred the power to elect and dismiss unit managers from party secretaries to the Workers' Congress. In fact, unit managers could be either elected by the workers or recruited through open advertisement. According to the 1988 Enterprise Laws proposed by the party's Central Committee and passed by the National People's Congress, the unit managers were granted, at least in theory, the power to control and manage their units without any interference from either party organizations or local government.[62] The implication was that the local party as an organization was being forced to take a back seat in economic affairs and was thereby losing its institutional cohesiveness in urban areas. It was, therefore, quite natural for party leaders at the bottom level to bitterly complain that "the power of the factory director [*chang zhang*] is real; the power of the party committee [*dang Wei*] is empty."[63]

By the late 1980s, the local and grass-roots party organizations had virtually lost their sense of mission and their reason for existence. They not only ceased to function as the basic unifying force of society serving to organize and mobilize the masses, they even encountered difficulties in conducting their own "organizational life" (*zuzhi shenghuo*). Traditionally, the "organizational life" had been guided through party meetings at frequent and regular intervals by all basic-level cells. It was designed to create consensus among party members and reach decisions for the implementation of instructions from above. By the early 1980s, however, party organizational life had become increasingly lax, or even nonexistent, in many areas. Leading cadres employed a variety of excuses to hold either fewer meetings or none at all. Many party members justified their nonattendance on the grounds of being too busy in implementing reform programs.[64] It was really true that because of the reform policies of pay linked to piecework production, the grass-roots party organizations were faced with tremendous difficulties in getting party members, who were already busy catching up with the assigned work, together to meet.[65]

Another indicator of the collapse of party discipline was that many party organizations could not, or would not even bother to, collect dues from members for months or years at a time.[66] As Hsi-Sheng Chi put it, "Poor discipline of party members had become a particularly onerous liability for the party in the 1980s. Even though the popular beliefs about the rectitude and honesty of the CCP's style of work in earlier decades had always been myth than reality, it is nevertheless true that party members were never as corrupt and dishonest as they have been under Deng's leadership."[67] The original spirit of the Chinese Communist Party, which had once called itself the "proletarian vanguard," has drastically decayed in the midst of a profound sociopolitical reform.

The top party leadership tried to rectify these "unhealthy trends" and boost morale within the party organizations by extolling the virtues of the new principle of the separation of party and state. In an important party document published in its official organ, *People's Daily*, in January 1988, the Central Committee of the CCP stated that under the new principle, the party would exercise "political leadership" over the state organs but would abdicate "organizational" or "operational" leadership. No sooner had this principle been adopted, however, than opposition emerged. Many party members argued that the separation of the party and state would undoubtedly reduce the party's power. Cadres who specialized in political work were particularly worried that the party's functions would be further reduced and that they as individual members, and the party organizations, would loose all power and prestige.[68]

Some individual party members even further damaged party's image and reputation, by engaging in "official profiteering." A typical example of this kind of scandal was the Hainan automobile-smuggling case, which shocked the entire country with the number and rank of the party members involved. This scandal, which was committed from January 1984 to March 1985, involved almost all the top-ranking cadres of the Hainan Administrative Region, including the deputy secretary of the Hainan regional party committee, Lei Yu. Using their privileges in the government and party, this group of cadres acquired huge amounts of foreign currency and bank loans to finance the importation of about 90,000 automobiles, numerous television sets, videocassette recorders, and motorcycles. Then they resold them, at a high profit, to other parties in China who lacked such privileges and access to these merchandise.[69] With this kind of corruption spreading nationwide, the major party organ, *Red Flag* (*Hongqi*), had to admit in 1986 that party members accounted for over two-thirds of all profiteering criminals, an astonishingly high percentage in view of the fact that party members constituted less than 4 percent of the general population at that time.[70] In fact, this figure did not even include the smugglers, many of whom were high-ranking cadres or their children.

In short, by the late 1980s, the basic-level party organizations had lost their "real power" and the momentum to direct productive activities and control the "political life" (*zhengzhi shenhuo*) of the people, or even the party membership. The party at the basic level ceased to function as the monolithic institutional fabric of the society—capable of mobilizing and inciting the masses, as it had done in the past decades. In addition, with the party losing its own institutional cohesiveness and political morale, its image had been damaged to the extent that many people frequently drew a parallel between the CCP of the late 1980s and the Guomindang of the late 1940s, because of their similar corruption. In the 1980s, as one China scholar observed, party leaders no longer led a selfless revolutionary vanguard; and the CCP as an organization had been drowned in the amenities of material well-being.[71]

The political and economic reforms not only weakened the party's leadership and its grass-roots organizations, but also led to the bankruptcy of the official ideology (Marxism-Leninism–Mao Zedong Thought). In the name of "emancipating thinking," in the late 1970s and the early 1980s Deng Xiaoping launched a campaign within the party and throughout the country to criticize Mao as a party leader and repudiate Mao Zedong Thought as the official ideology.[72] His original intent behind the campaign had been to eradicate ideological obstacles, such as some of Mao's thought (the official ideology at the time), to his reform programs. However, he did not anticipate such a negative consequence as the loss of the strong official ideology, which he and the current leadership now desperately needed to regain in order to sustain the regime.

Treading in the steps of Deng Xiaoping, the party's propaganda organs went a step further by questioning the applicability of Marxism and Leninism, which had been seen as the ideological and theoretical bases of Mao Zedong Thought in the past decades. For instance, the *People's Daily* in a commentary in 1984, told the populace that orthodox Marxist-Leninist theory was obsolete and that its rigid application (such as Mao's Thought) could no longer solve China's problems.[73] It said, "we cannot expect the writings of Marx and Lenin written in their time to solve all of our present problems."[74] A year later, when addressing a group of visiting Italian Communist party officials, then party chief Hu Yaobang said that in order to develop Marxism, its "outdated theories must be rejected," and "the latest achievements of all humanity must be incorporated into it."[75]

The officially initiated downgrading or "demystification" of Marxism-Leninism-Mao Zedong Thought as the official ideology was warmly welcomed by many liberally inclined theorists and by people both within and outside the party. For instance, writing under the pseudonym, Ma Ding, a lecturer at Nanjing University published an article in November 1985 in which he argued that the works of Marx were more a critique of capitalism than a blueprint for building socialism, especially the "socialism in the Chinese style." Moreover, Ma argued that he found no ready answers in Marxism to existing problems in contemporary China. He further pointed out that even Marx had given credit to some "bourgeois economists," such as Adam Smith and David Recardo.[76] Some of the liberal theorists went even further in charging that Mao was wrong in insisting on implementing concepts such as "absolute egalitarianism," which stifled "people's enthusiasm for work" and sanctioned "laziness and shoddy work."[77]

In addition to the questioning of Marxism-Maoism's continued relevance to contemporary China, those liberal theorists who were reform-minded also began to criticize the very method of studying Marxism, arguing that the "dogmatic and repetitive teaching methods" in the universities and high schools must be changed.[78] They called attention to the indifference and apathy to Marxism-Maoism studies among high school and university students, pointing out that some universities, like the prestigious Beijing University

(Beida), had decided to reduce study time on the official ideology by as much as 30 to 40 percent.[79]

The attack on the original official ideology, which was made by the new leadership based on considerations of political expediency and by the liberal activists, who had called for greater freedom of thought, brought about among the people a profound "crisis of faith" in socialism and "crisis of confidences" in the future of the country (plus a crisis of trust in the party-state, the three crises were popularly called *sanxin weiji*—the crises of the three faiths). Many people, and even party members in the midst of the political and economic reforms, lost their "spiritual pillar" (*jingshen zhizhu*), which had been incarnated as Marxism-Leninism-Mao Zedong Thought and had guided them to support, and even sacrifice for, the Communist totalitarian regime. They simply could not make any sense out of the ossified political philosophy in the context of the drastic sociopolitical changes brought about by Deng's leadership. Peng Zeng, a high-ranking orthodox hard-liner in the party, once complained that Deng's liberal associates "disturbed people's mind" (*raoluan renxin*) and "confused the matter of principle," so that people lost the direction and motives to construct socialism in China.[80]

Confronted with such crises of faith, during the decade of 1978–1988, the party leaders made several valiant efforts to reverse the trends in the decline of "faith" and "confidence" among the masses and party members by adjusting their political reasoning to accommodate current policy needs. Deng's personal contribution to this effort was exemplified by his famous dictum, "White cat or black cat, the cat that catches mice is a good cat," which is a vivid portrait of his pragmatism. For Deng and his associates, so long as the two related sociopolitical goals—economic prosperity and strong party leadership—could be achieved, any necessary means should be implemented, including the "responsibility system," the "market mechanism," and the "separation of party and state." In short, to obtain higher living standards for the people and abundant wealth for the society is the major objective of "socialism with Chinese characteristics." How was the nation to become wealthy? Deng's answer was that the Chinese should "dare to practice" without being constrained by any predetermined ideological principles: "Practice is the only criterion of truth." However, all these efforts to reverse the "unhealthy" trends corroding people's "faith" and "confidence" in the party-state seemed to have done no more than providing a short-term tranquilizer. "Practice" was "doing" rather than "guiding." It can never replace the functions of an ideology, which are to legitimize the regime and mobilize the people. In addition, the result of the "practice" of the reforms could not possibly satisfy everybody. While millionaires cropped up in the cities as well as the villages, many other people suffered from the reforms. But, unless the disadvantaged could maintain their "faith in socialism" and "confidence in the future," they would resent the reform policies and even the current regime.

The basis of the problem was that after the old official ideology had been shattered, Deng and his followers proved unable to advance a new one. The functions of the old ideology were replaced only with several pragmatic and near-sighted principles, such as the goal to "get rich" by "practicing" any pragmatic policies. Such principles can never substitute for the functions of an official ideology to guide and reassure people in the long run.

In sum, by the late 1980s, the economic and political reforms initiated by Deng Xiaoping and his supporters actually had brought about a dual consequence: economic growth and political instability. The reforms themselves were designed by the leadership as the means to solidify their political power to control the party and state under the post–Cultural Revolution sociopolitical conditions. Once they gained their own momentum, however, the reforms seemed to leave the leaders with only one choice: improving the economy or losing political power. As a Western diplomat in Beijing pointed out, "The party can claim credit for enormous economic improvement, but if you've got only one horse to ride—the economic horse—and it stumbles, you've got nowhere to go. People in the Communist party are united by the sense that they have to deliver economically or they'll be out."[81] Before, the party could use the official ideology to gain popular support and employ the party organization to mobilize the people, as it had done even during the 1959–1962 economic catastrophe following the "Great Leap Forward." Now, however, the party could only "bet on one horse"—an economic miracle. Deng himself admitted: "Without improving the living standard of the people, we'll have no future."[82]

NOTES

1. These two terms were often used by officials of the time to address Mao Zedong and Chinese Communist Party.

2. See Wei Jingsheng, "The Fifth Modernization: Democracy and Etc.," *Beijing zhi Chun* (Beijing Spring), October 1993, p. 17.

3. Ibid., p. 18.

4. See Andrew J. Nathan, *Chinese Democracy* (New York: Alfred A. Knopf, 1985), p. 92.

5. See Immanuel C. Y. Hsu, *China without Mao: The Search for a New Order*, 2nd ed. (New York: Oxford University Press, 1990), pp. 215–216.

6. Ibid., p. 216.

7. The script of "River Elegy" is excerpted in *Zhonguo zhi Chun* (China Spring), Jan. and Feb. 1989, pp. 36–69.

8. Yu Xiguang, Li Liangdong and Ni Jianshong, *Dachao xinqi: Deng Xiaoping nanxun qianqian houhou* (Tidal Wave: Before and after Deng Xiaoping's Tour in Southern China) (Beijing: Press of Chinese Broadcast and Television, 1992), p. 24.

9. Ibid.

10. Tang Tsou, "Back from the Brink of Revolutionary 'Feudal' Totalitarianism," in Victor Nee and David Mozingo, eds., *State and Society in Contemporary China* (Ithaca, N.Y.: Cornell University Press, 1983), p. 53.

11. See Central Committee of the Chinese Communist Party, "Communiqué of the Third Plenum of the Eleventh Central Committee of the Communist Party of China," *Beijing Review*, December 29, 1978, p. 8.

12. Yu, Li, and Ni, *Spring Tide*, p. 24.

13. See *Shiyijie sanzhong quanhui yilai zhongyao wenxian xuandu* (Selected Readings of Major Documents since the Third Plenum of the Eleventh Central Committee) (Beijing: People's Press, 1979), pp. 2–16.

14. Tsou, "Back from the Brink," p. 53.

15. *Hongqi* (Red Flag) 3 (September 1977): 18.

16. Deng Xiaoping, *Deng Xiaoping Wenxuan:1975–1982* (Selected Works of Deng Xiaoping: 1975–1982) (Beijing: People's Press, 1983), p. 133.

17. Hu Fuming, "Practice Is the Sole Criterion for Testing Truth," *Guangming Ribao*, May 11, 1978.

18. *Peking Review*, June 23, 1978, pp. 14–21.

19. Ibid.

20. Central Committee of the Chinese Communist Party, *Communiqué of the Third Plenary Session of the Eleventh Central Committee of the Chinese Communist Party* (Beijing: People's Daily Press, 1978), pp. 14–15.

21. Ibid., p. 15.

22. *Ming Bao Monthly* (Hong Kong), November 30, 1978, p. 1.

23. *Beijing Review*, July 6, 1981, p. 33.

24. "Deng: Cleaning Up Mao's Feudal Mistakes," *Guardian*, September 21, 1980, p. 16

25. "Had 'Cultural Revolution' Mass Support?" *Beijing Review*, November 23, 1981, pp. 20–21.

26. Ibid.

27. See Wei Hongyun, *Zhongguo Jindai Shi:1919–1949* (A Modern History of China: 1919–1949) (Harbin, China: Harbin People's Press, 1982).

28. For Deng's speech, see Deng, *Selected Works*, pp. 280–302.

29. Concerning "political restructuring," see "Deng Calls for Speedup in Reform," *Beijing Review*, August 24, 1987, p. 15.

30. Ibid., p. 290.

31. Deng Xiaoping, *Selected Works*, p. 289.

32. See ibid.

33. See Yu, Li, and Ni, *Tidal Wave*, pp. 80–81.

34. This probably is the reason why the new party chief, Jiang Zemin, began to concurrently hold the position as the Chairman of the government in 1993.

35. See Yu, Li, and Ni, *Tidal Wave*, p. 17.

36. Central Committee of the Chinese Communist Party, "Communiqué of the Third Plenum of the Eleventh Central Committee," p. 12.

37. See "Several Questions in Strengthening and Perfecting the Production Responsibility System for Agricultural Production," *Issues and Studies* 5 (May 1981): 77–82; See also "Rural Contract," *Beijing Review*, November 10, 1980, pp. 5–6.

38. "A Program for Current Agricultural Work," *Beijing Review*, June 14, 1982, p. 21.

39. James C. F. Wang, *Contemporary Chinese Politics: An Introduction* (Englewood Cliffs, N.J.: Prentice Hall, 1993), p. 259.

40. See Colin Mackerras and Amanda Yorke, *The Cambridge Handbook of Contemporary China* (New York: Cambridge University Press, 1991), pp. 156–159.

41. See Yu, Li, and Ni, *Spring Tide*, p. 58.

42. Ibid., pp. 58–59.

43. See ibid., pp. 63–64.

44. *Beijing Review*, October 29, 1984, p. vi.

45. Ibid.

46. See Yu, Li, and Ni, *Spring Tide*, pp. 63–64.

47. *Beijing Review*, December 29, 1986, p. 18.

48. Ibid.

49. See Yu, Li, and Ni, *Spring Tide*, p. 251.

50. Ibid., p. 248.

51. Chao Zenyao, *Yongdong de dachao: Zhonggou shichang jingji daguan* (Gigantic wave: An overview of China's market economy) (Xian, China: Northwest University Press, 1993), p. 46.

52. Ibid., p. 42.

53. Ibid., p. 43.

54. "China's Capital Goods Market," *Beijing Review*, November 1989, p. 20.

55. Dwight H. Perkins, "The Prospects for China's Economic Reforms," in Anthony J. Kane, ed., *China Briefing, 1990* (Boulder, Colo.: Westview Press, 1990), p. 37.

56. Chao, *Gigantic Wave*, pp. 49–50.

57. Concerning the growth rate of GNP, see *Renmin Ribao* (*People's Daily*), September 25, 1993.

58. See Deng, *Selected Works*, pp. 280–302; Yu, Li, and Ni, *Spring Tide*, pp. 80–81; for discussion of his directives, see also, the first section of this chapter.

59. See Deng, *Selected Works*, p. 289.

60. See John Burns, "Local Cadre Accommodation to the 'Responsibility System' in Rural China," *Pacific Affairs* 4 (Winter 1985–1986): 614, 617.

61. See *Beijing Review*, October 29, 1984, pp. i–xvi.

62. Wang Baoliang, Chen Guoyao, and Liu Mingpuo, *Zhonggou zai sikao: '92 da xieshi* (China Rethinking: '92 Portrait) (Beijing: People's Press, 1992), pp. 54–58.

63. *Xue Lilun* (Study Theory) 217 (1984): 24.

64. *People's Daily*, January 28, 1983, p. 4.

65. Ibid., February 16, 1985, p. 3.

66. Ibid., June 7, 1982, p. 2.

67. Hsi-sheng Ch'i, *Politics of Disillusionment: The Chinese Communist Party under Deng Xiaoping, 1978–1989* (Armonk, N.Y.: M. E. Sharpe, 1991), p. 262.

68. *People's Daily*, January 2, 1988, p. 4.

69. Ibid., August 1, 1985.

70. *Hongqi* (Red Flag) 23 (October 1986): 16.

71. Dwight Perkins, "The Prospects for China's Economic Reforms," p. 41.

72. See "Communiqué of the Third Plenum of the Eleventh Central Committee of the CCP," *Peking Review*, December 29, 1987, pp. 14–15; see also, the first section of this chapter.

73. *People's Daily*, December 7, 1984, p. 1.

74. Ibid.

75. *Beijing Review*, August 30, 1985, p. 20.

76. *Beijing Review*, July 13, 1986, p. 20.

77. See Liu Guoguang, "Socialism Is Not Egalitarianism," *Beijing Review*, September 28, 1987, pp. 16–18.

78. *People's Daily*, February 17, 1986.

79. Ibid.

80. *Far Eastern Economic Review*, February 11, 1986, p. 5.

81. Charles Radin, "Communism's Longevity Rests on Economy," *Denver Post*, June 13, 1993.

82. Ibid.

4

The Meaning of June 4, 1989

June 4, 1989 was a prime example of civil disobedience under an authoritarian regime, an eruption of emotions—frustration, indignation, and both disillusionment and hope on the part of the people and anger and fear on the part of an insecure government. Circumstances helped create the most tragic drama in the history of the People's Republic. However, in the sound and fury one can perceive much more. To a great extent, the incident was a tragic showdown between an nascent civil society, characterized by aggressiveness and high ideals, and a waning regime with a determination to hold on to power. By inflicting serious injuries on both sides of the confrontation, the tragedy had tremendous, perhaps traumatic impact on the ruling party and the Chinese people, especially the urban intellectuals. The outcome of the conflict has subsequently helped define the course of sociopolitical development in China.

China pundits in the West, and especially in the United States, while decrying the brutality of the Chinese government, went to great lengths in analyzing the details of the 1989 tragedy. Some Western observers emphasized the dynamics of the power struggle. The shortcoming of such an approach is its "inability to explain how factional modes of conflict interact with other modes" especially the role of the people and the interplay between public sentiments and the elite politics of the ruling party.[1] We do recognize factionalism as an integral part of politics in mainland China, even today. What we are interested in is how such a factional struggle, which, while certainly having its own dynamics, interacted with various social and political forces. The drama of Tiananmen in 1989 was thus not only "another instance of a force outside the factional system . . . erupting into the political arena in an attempt to end the factions' monopoly of politics, and of the factions closing ranks to protect their joint position," but rather an instance of the intricate relationship between the CCP elite politics and the changing socio-cultural trends.[2]

THE IMPENDING CRISIS

The backdrop of the 1989 crisis was complex, involving economic as well as political elements and foreign as well as domestic factors. Like many major political crises in world history, the tragedy of 1989 in Beijing was triggered by an ailing economy following the ten years of reform. After years of bullish growth, China's economy began to show signs of great trouble starting in 1988. Deng Xiaoping's "groping strategy" (wading across the river by finding stepping-stones) and Zhao Ziyang's improvizations, such as the "primary stage of socialism," produced unexpected problems.

In the farming sector, where the post–Mao regime had scored impressive victories through the household responsibility system, the speed of progress slowed. Between 1985 and 1988, China's industry grew at a rate of 17.8 percent per year, whereas its agriculture rose by only 3.9 percent annually. Grain output per capita even dropped slightly.[3]

Such a slowdown resulted from a variety of reasons. For one thing, China's farm land per capita is among the smallest in the world. In densely populated areas in the east, there was apparently a limit to agricultural growth. Moreover, the burgeoning market economy discouraged the production of grains which yielded less profit than cash crops. It also encouraged exploitive farming techniques, especially heavy uses of chemical fertilizers, which produced immediate advantages but were detrimental to the soil's long-term productivity. Healthy agricultural growth was made more difficult by the avaricious middlemen whose speculation raised the prices of production inputs such as fertilizers sky-high.[4] To the alarm of the Beijing government, China's farmland was being devoured by urban development at a frightening speed, while the growth of the rural population was getting out of hand. Moreover, since the implementation of the contract system, which replaced the wasteful group labor under the people's commune system, millions of Chinese farmers flocked into the cities to seek temporary employment. In contrast to the years of readjustment of the early 1960s when 2 million Chinese workers were sent back to the countryside from where they had come, the government in the 1980s had no way to stop the migration and the fluidity of the population only added to the stress in the cities.

Reform in the Chinese cities and the industrial sector proved much more complicated. Certainly, the post–Mao reform opened up unprecedented opportunities in the cities. But in the period up to 1989, many serious problems developed that led to popular discontent. One of these problems was the *guandao*, or official profiteering, which at once enraged and alarmed people. Through legal and extra-legal means, officials and their relatives turned various government departments into a money-making machine. Most notorious of all was the so-called crown-prince party (*taizi dang*), children of high-ranking officials in the CCP and the government who reaped huge profits by virtue of their ties with various governmental agencies. The stories about Deng Xiaoping's son, Deng Pufang, who controlled the Chinese Foundation of the Handicapped and later the Kanghua Corporation, and Zhao Ziyang's son, Zhao Dajun, who made a huge fortune in South China, were well known.[5] They brought the Chinese art of speculation to a new height and their affluence made a mockery of the much-publicized Four Cardinal Principles. Hu Yaobang was not exaggerating when he said in 1981 that the CCP was more corrupt than the GMD in the 1940s.[6] In 1989, rampant corruption totally shattered the people's faith in the ruling party's "self-correcting capability."

The party, having long ago lost its revolutionary edge, became more disoriented than ever as cadres at all levels behaved like a "swarm of headless flies, buzzing around in every direction." The collapse of self-confidence originated at the very top of the CCP. A good indicator was the great number of high-ranking officials' children studying in Western countries, especially the U.S., with some already holding green cards.[7] As a result, "those who are closest to the leadership" became the "most pessimistic in China." They did not believe a word the leaders said.[8]

In fact, the CCP had never found an armor to resist what Mao called the "sugar-coated bullets." The post–Mao glasnost only helped ideologically disarm the party apparatus, despite Deng Xiaoping's warning at several occasions against the "unhealthy trends" in the party. There were still some officials, Deng observed in 1984, who regarded themselves as "masters rather than servants of the people" and used their positions to seek "personal privileges." This practice, he warned the party, had "aroused strong resentment among the masses and tarnished the party's credibility."[9] By and large, however, his words fell on deaf ears.

For reformers who aimed to marketize the Chinese economy, the most thorny question involved the thousands of China's state-owned enterprises. While all kinds of private businesses, both Chinese- and foreign-owned, prospered as a result of the government's preferential treatment in taxing and pricing, state-owned enterprises found it hard to break the shackles of the planned economy. They had to pay high taxes and sell the products at set prices. Employees in such enterprises had little incentive, as their bonuses were artificially limited by various regulations.

Unfortunately, reformers in the Chinese government paid little heed to the plight of the state-owned enterprises, which possessed over 60 percent of China's industrial capacity. Until 1989 their measures in dealing with the public sector of industry, such as the introduction of share holding (*gufenhua*) or separation of government and enterprises (*zheng qi fenkai*) did little to alleviate the problem.[10] Workers in the state-owned factories naturally found it hard to go along with the reform. A significant portion of industrial workers felt the pinch of economic stagnation in 1988–1989. In the major cities, drivers of the public transit system expressed their grievances by failing to adhere to the schedule, while sit-in strikes were used by factory workers to send a message to the government about their feelings about inflation and unfair wage and bonus regulations.[11]

Unable to solve the problem of low productivity, the government decided to get rid of unprofitable enterprises by implementing the bankruptcy law. Many workers were laid off with subsistence pay and, in 1988, 15 to 20 million workers were underemployed.[12] Tension thus mounted between the workers and the managerial class, and some desperate workers resorted to violence as a way to resolve disputes. Underlying the tension was the workers' loss of pride and prestige and the sense of insecurity under a government that claimed to be proletarian. Few could miss the irony.

The plight of the urban population was further aggravated by double-digit inflation in 1988 and 1989 (19 percent in 1988 and 28 percent in the first quarter of 1989), which magnified the gap between the rich and poor. The salaried class was hit hard. Even according to official statistics, real income of urban families declined by 35 percent in 1988 and in early 1989, there was no sign of improvement.[13]

In addition, there was the phenomenon of *naoti-daogua* ("brain-workers" make less money than "muscle-workers"). The average income of intellectuals was 10 percent lower than that of the workers. College professors, school teachers, and ordinary government employees found it increasingly difficult to make ends meet. When the honor they received for their dedication and contribution did not turn into material betterment, it was said that they felt as if they were being "carried in a sedan chair without their pants on." While this joke betrayed a profound bitterness among China's educated elite, the hard truth was that according to top secret sources, the average life expectancy of China's intellectuals was only fifty-eight, ten years shorter than the national average. 31.8 percent of the intellectuals died between the ages of forty and fifty. A full 50 percent died of cancer.[14]

It is worth noting nevertheless that the extent of economic malaise never even approached some of the difficult periods in China's past. Unlike the late 1950s, when millions of Chinese citizens died of starvation, and the 1970s, when China was a characterized as a nation of "blue ants," there was neither serious famine nor material scarcity in the late 1980s. What distinguished China in the 1980s from China before the post–Mao reform was the Chinese people's greater independence from the party apparatus and their higher expectations of government.

Indeed, like any other political crisis, the Tiananmen Incident of 1989 occurred in a volatile political and social atmosphere. Many Chinese, and especially the educated elite, had become restless in the beginning of 1989 for they believed the reform had entered a deadlock, primarily as a result of resistance from the political establishment. At the same time, the retreat of the ruling party in ideological and cultural spheres left enough room for their limited free expression. In the provinces as well as in Beijing, college students organized forums on current affairs and intellectuals gathered at their salons, discussing political as well as nonpolitical issues. Newspaper editors began to openly identify with the interests of the local people rather than the will of the CCP. Democracy, or some sort of democratic mechanism, was considered a remedy to the floundering leadership of the Communist party. The mushrooming of associations, clubs, and informal gatherings indicated a growing hope, illusory as it might have been, that the citizens could to oblige the party and the government, through nonviolent means, to accept changes that would foster political democracy and economic freedom.[15]

Underlying the agitation and restless was an ever-deepening faith crisis—the educated elite had not only become apathetic to the political orthodoxy but more vocal in opposing it. For the increasingly discontented intelligentsia, while the rigid CCP ideology had long become a straightjacket on Chinese thinking, the party machine simply lacked the creativity and daring to break away from it. Outright repudiation of Marxism-Leninism and Mao Zedong Thought being still too dangerous a thing to do, leading intellectuals tried to open wider space for public opinion when the political establishment became disoriented.

The deep anxiety found a most powerful vehicle in *He Shang* (River Elegy) a television series produced by a group of daring young men. In a powerful language and through stunning montages, the *Elegy* magnified the debilitating power of China's cultural heritage while scratching the surface of the country's political inertia. The authors boldly suggested that the emulation of the maritime civilization and a continuous openness held the key to China's rejuvenation.[16] *He Shang* was by no means definitive about Chinese culture, let alone the nation's future. But with a theme reminiscent of the May 4th of 1919, the authors were invoking the ghosts of "Mr. Democracy" and "Mr. Modernization." For our purposes, the most important thing about *He Shang* was not the accuracy of its data or even the power of its artistic presentation. What is most impressive is the profound sense of anxiety on the part of its authors about China's state of crisis and the tremendous popularity of the series among the Chinese, especially the intellectuals.[17]

For many intellectuals, the message of *He Shang* was a genuine concern for the nation at a critical juncture of its history. It fit well the general mood since 1986 and their acute awareness that the reform had entered a period of stalemate. At any rate, the euphoria in the early stage of reform was replaced by worry, and accentuated by some mind-boggling facts. For example, Song Jian, director of the State Science and Technology Commission, reported that despite the growth in the early 1980s, China's per capita GNP still ranked among the poorest 20 nations in a study of 126 countries. It was only 1/27 of that of Japan, 1/33 of that of the United States. Nine of China's most backward provinces were comparable to Chad, which was at the bottom of the list.[18] While Zhao

Ziyang's think tank invented the term "primary stage of socialism," which was made official at the Thirteenth Congress of the CCP to pave the way for an even more radical deviation from the political orthodoxy, such statistics were enough to make many intellectuals restless.

On the other hand, the situation was by no means bleak. Deng Xiaoping's pragmatism and popular search for prosperity, while creating enormous confusion among the ruling party, led to a relatively relaxed environment in which people could reinterpret Marxism outside its formerly defined boundaries. Far-sighted Communists also recognized the need for a certain degree of freedom of thought and speech. In the early 1980s, Hu Yaobang, then secretary-general of the CCP, guaranteed that intellectuals would not receive any political reprisal for what they said in academic debates or literary writings. Most intellectuals preferred a reformist approach to solving China's political problems. When influential intellectuals such as Fang Lizhi encouraged the youth to join the CCP, he was not alone in hoping to help China turn the corner by changing the composition of the ruling party. Change from the top down and reform within the socialist framework, however infeasible, held tremendous appeal to China's intelligentsia.[19]

With its powerful medium, *He Shang* accentuated a type of discourse in pre-Tiananmen China characterized by a daring questioning of the status quo. Operating in the peculiar political culture of China, the discourse sought to open a new horizon of dialogue between the cultural elite and the political elite, and also between the elite and the masses. In a time of ideological quandary, frustration stimulated further search for new solutions. Before 1989, three schools of thought were most articulate. The first, represented by the Academy of Chinese Culture (*Zhougguo wenhua shuyuan*), was undoubtedly a backlash to the Communist culture, which had its roots in the cultural iconoclasm of the May 4 period. The second school, which advocated by young intellectuals such as Gan Yang, aimed at changing Chinese culture by infusing it with Western values. The third was the most influential. Led by scholars such as Su Shaozhi and Jin Guantao, the school gathered a number of young scholars whose viewpoints found a powerful medium in a number of publications of which *Toward the Future* and *China and the World* were avidly read by educated Chinese, especially college students. Thus starting in the early 1980s, new values and theories inundated Chinese college campuses and book stores, helping to produce an intellectual climate that was defiant toward the Communist ideology and critical of China's cultural heritage.[20]

The result was a "New Enlightenment" fueled by a reaction to the cultural obscurantism of the CCP. The discussion of new, largely Western ideas was not only fashionable, it represented a sincere effort to bring China from its largely self-imposed isolation into the international community. Except within a small segment of the political establishment, Marxism-Leninism and Mao Zedong Thought had long ago ceased to be a matter of interest in the people's daily life.

In most work units, political studies were either abandoned or preserved in form only. While political cadres lost much prestige and power, the class of technocrats ascended, to the chagrin of their less educated rivals. However, the conservatives in the party and at all levels of government would not give in without a battle. At the same time, the reformers among the technocrats, who were smarting from wounds inflicted during the Cultural Revolution, dared not be too aggressive for fear of retaliation from their disgruntled rivals. The problem with such a compromise was that it led to political stagnation which fed the public unrest and its desire to pursue a remedy for China's ailments.

The younger generation, and especially college students enjoyed the opportunity of openness (*kaifang*) for not only were bookstores stocked with books on new ideas, classrooms, too, allowed some free thinking. The older students, who had experienced the political culture of persecution of the Cultural Revolution, were eager to summarize the lessons of the ten years of great destruction. Hu Ping's treatise "On the Freedom of Speech" spoke for many of the Lost Generation. The younger students, who had no memory of the Maoist era, were eager to express their views which, although immature and vague, often deviated from the official line.

The New Enlightenment created a very fluid intellectual atmosphere in which "everybody was fueling the society; few worked on its brakes." When Zhao Ziyang called for the building of a "socialist new order," no New Enlightenment advocates responded. Almost none of these knights for sweeping changes was expert in law, ethics, or public administration.[21] In front of the intellectual ferment and reformist agitation was the seemingly immutable political order, its inertia nurtured by an era of tight political control. The reformers and their supporters found no way to get around it. Thus, despite claims of new solutions, Chinese society, and especially the intellectual elite, was still clouded by a profound sense of loss, which threatened to become cultural nihilism and political radicalism.

Theoreticians in the CCP proved impressionable in regard to the sentiments of the educated elite. Historical circumstances and changing public sentiment not only gave the pathfinders in the party an opportunity to search for new ways to interpret orthodox Marxism-Leninism, but actually impelled them to find ways to rejuvenate the party. The Anti-Bourgeois Liberalization Campaign of 1986 ironically did not restore the one-voice hall (*yiyan tang*), as might have been expected, simply because the party ideologues offered no answer to the myriad of problems and because the party machine had never recovered from the fatal blow of the CR. Unable to jettison its restraining mode of thinking, the party tried helplessly to stop the onslaught of ideological imports, only to find it had run out of theoretical ammunition.

Until April 1989, reformers in the party were able to get their ideas across to the Chinese people through the official organs, especially the *People's Daily*, which was more lively than *Zhongyang Ribao* (*Central Daily*), its counterpart in Taiwan. *Shijie Jingji Daobao* (World Economy Herald) in Shanghai often served as a scout in advocating reforms. On many crucial issues, articles in the *Herald* constantly tested the limits of reform. Unable, and perhaps unwilling, to negate Marxism-Leninism, most advocates of reform tried to blaze a trail by attacking dogmatism in a Dengist fashion. Su Shaozhi, director of the Institute of Marxism-Leninism and Mao Zedong Thought in the Chinese Academy of Social Sciences, called for the creative development of Marxism and attributed the people's disillusionment with the official ideology to dogmatism within the party.[22] The more radical intellectuals blamed the chaos in economic reform on a lack of democracy. To them, "unconditional freedom of speech," which gave the people an active role in politics, was the remedy to problems such as official corruption. Wang Ruoshui's writing on alienation under socialism for the first time called for changes far beyond what the party chiefs would allow. He was, in effect, demanding an end to the one-party rule of the CCP.[23]

CRYING OUT

Public sentiment in early 1989 was thus just like a heap of dried firewood waiting for a spark. Then, in April, Hu Yaobang, the ousted former secretary-general of the CCP (1979–1986) died at a most inopportune moment. A Chinese farmer in Sichuan might not even have known who he was, but for millions of the educated and urban population, Hu's death was a great loss since he had no doubt been the last starry-eyed idealist and the greatest liberal in the CCP establishment.[24] A man of tremendous moral courage and intellectual capacity, he led the campaign of "bringing order out of chaos" that restored the morale of the party and government by rehabilitating thousands of persecuted cadres and intellectuals. He also championed the battle against CR obscurantism and attempted to rejuvenate scientific socialism by "seeking truth from facts." In fact, Deng's return to power was largely the work of Hu, who remained Deng's number one confidant until 1986, when he offended Deng by naively taking the latter's promise to retire at face value and by tolerating what hardliners called "bourgeois liberalization." Deng betrayed his younger ally by conceding to other old men in the party, and he forced the loyal Hu to resign through a process that violated the party's constitution. However, no one expected that Hu's sudden death would set off the greatest and most tragic popular protest in China's history.

Following Hu's death, discontented students turned the funeral into a protest against the gerontocracy and rampant corruption in the government. Many of the slogans were directed at Deng Xiaoping and other old men in the party. The protest was dramatically staged on April 22 by three students who knelt on the steps in front of the Great Hall of the People in which Hu's funeral was being held. The visit by Soviet leader Mikhail Gorbachev and the presence of an international news corps in Beijing, moreover, gave extra impetus to the activism of a new generation of Chinese students.

The students' demands for political reform and further democratization of the government apparently had a substantial social and political background. When they took to the streets in 1989, they were doing the same thing as their predecessors had done in 1895, 1919, 1935, and 1946. They were assuming their moral responsibility for the nation at a critical moment of its fate. They were also in a unique position because, apart from the political establishment, they were undoubtedly the best-organized group in Chinese society. In a society where the power of religion was minimal, college campuses naturally became the centers of social conscience as well as intellectual enlightenment. A sense of mission, not unlike that of the Confucian literati, called the youth to step forward to protest, on behalf of the people, against a new parasitic class and break the government's lethargy. Many protestors naively believed that their noble action would move the entire nation to break the deadlock in Zhongnanhai. Most significant of all, for the first time in the history of the people's republic, they put forward the demand for the democratization of the political system.

Without a political program of their own, the students nevertheless found a grand stage for their youthful dreams.

What is democracy: Now that the people's minds are awakened, an excellent opportunity has arisen. We want to make this foundation even better. What is democracy: Democracy is where the people are in control of the political power, and not political power controlling the people. [Democracy is present when] the people can choose their own political and economic life according to their wishes. Democracy is taking these glorious democratic ideas and instilling them in the minds of every citizen of the republic. We did not do this very well in the past; our education has been poor. The educational level of our children is very low, the educational level of our citizens is also very low. Our responsibility is to raise this level.[25]

Throughout the standoff, the students' demands, revolving around a government-citizen dialogue and governmental action against the *guandao*, were reasonable and, indeed, modest. They believed, in their political innocence, that they were speaking for the disenfranchised and their goals represented the future of China. Their show of patriotism, which was quickly reported around the world, did move millions of people, Chinese and foreigners alike.

The students' protest might have subsided had the Chinese government handled the crisis more patiently. But an editorial in the April 26th issue of *People's Daily* which labeled the protest as *dongluan* (turmoil) poured fuel on the fire. The very next day students took to streets again, totally ignoring the threat from the government. To further push forward their demand for a dialogue with the government leaders, the students started a hunger strike and by occupying Tiananmen Square, they totally ruined the much publicized summit between Deng Xiaoping and Mikhail Gorbachev. Deng Xiaoping certainly would not let such insult go unpunished.

The students' parade on April 27 was hailed by many residents of Beijing, including thousands of industrial workers. On May 17, more than a million people from all walks of life showed support for the hunger strikers in Tiananmen Square and demanded Deng's retirement and Li Peng's step-down. For the first time since 1978, slogans in great numbers were directed at Deng.[26] Similar demonstrations broke out simultaneously in some thirty other cities. Besides major cities such as Tianjin, Shanghai, and Chengdu, medium-sized cities such as Xiangtan, Mao Zedong's birth place, and Yanan, the Red capital during World War II, also witnessed student protests.[27]

Deng Xiaoping and the other old men in the CCP were well aware of the political implications of the demonstration, which was reminiscent of the April 5 Incident of 1976. Hu's popularity deeply hurt their feelings. However, they could find a larger bigger rationale—and rightfully so—for their obstinacy. When the hardliners condemned the students' action in the April 26 *People's Daily* editorial as *dongluan* the whole demonstration became depicted as the work of "a small minority of people with ulterior motives." The threatening tone of the conspiracy thesis virtually blocked the way for constructive dialogue between the government and demonstrators.[28]

As was the case in 1986, popular protest helped magnify the cracks in the political establishment. The students' determination and the hardliners' stubbornness confronted Zhao Ziyang, secretary general of the CCP, with a very difficult choice between his conscience and the will of the party elders. Until 1989, Zhao walked a political tightrope between the exigencies of economic reform and the almost impossible task of holding the party together. In 1987, Zhao joined the faction of the elders to oust Hu Yaobang, his erstwhile ally. Obviously, he sacrificed Hu to preserve his career as well as the economic reform. Hu's indiscretion in talking about political reforms increased both popular agitation and reaction from the conservatives, thus disrupting Zhao's economic goals. Shortly after Hu's disgrace, Zhao trumpeted Deng Xiaoping's two basic points, i.e., to uphold the Four Cardinal Principles and oppose "bourgeois liberalization" in politics and to continue the economic reform and openness, with a view to placating the still grumbling party elders. In fact his ideas on economy were most like those of Deng and starting in the 1980s, Zhao replaced Deng as the chief engineer to orchestrate China's reforms.

In 1988, Zhao's supporters began to advocate what they called "new authoritarianism" in order to avert the chaos that public agitation for rapid political reform would effect. Su Shaozhi, a member of Zhao's think tank, was heard to have said that the rule by man was necessary in the framework of the rule by law.[29] The slogan appealed to many Chinese who dreaded disorder because of their memory of the tumultuous Cultural Revolution and who yearned for material betterment in a politically stable environment. The approach was risky, though, for without the necessary political reform, establishment of channels for public grievances, and development of mechanisms to check political privileges, the new authoritarianism contributed to rampant corruption and public discontent. The race between economic growth and corruption was on, and the Zhao Ziyang camp was hoping that the former would outpace the latter, thus ensuring the fate of the reform.[30] Such a mind-set betrays the weakness of the reformers in relation to the political establishment.

Zhao's position in the CCP hierarchy was already shaky in 1988 when his reform began to fall apart. In early 1989, an undercurrent of sentiment to oust Zhao came into the open, pushed forward by elderly hardliners such as Chen Yun, Bo Yibo, Wang Zhen, Hu Qiaomu, Li Xiannian, and Peng Zhen. Bitter about their loss of prestige since the early 1980s, they blamed Zhao for the economic chaos and what they called "bourgeois liberalization." In 1989, when the reform was producing undesired results, Li Peng, the premier and the mouthpiece of the conservatives, threw barbs at Zhao again. In his report to the Second Session of the Seventh National People's Congress, Li suggested that the chaos in China's economy, which was responsible for the loss of the people's in the government, was produced by the rashness of the reform and a disregard for China's peculiar situation.[31]

When the Tiananmen standoff began, Zhao was paying a visit to North Korea. As soon as he returned, he came under pressure directly from Deng Xiaoping to deal with the students harshly. This time, however, Zhao Ziyang did not want to be used as Deng Xiaoping's weapon. Rather, he adopted a moderate approach to dealing with the students and endorsed their demand for a dialogue. He even tried, through his top aides, to establish contact with the student leaders. Unfortunately the students did not trust him and ignored his hints. No one can know exactly what was on Zhao's mind in those heart-wrenching days, but his decision to break with Deng Xiaoping at the height of the crisis forms an enduring chapter in the history of the CCP. Politically, Zhao Ziyang probably did the right thing in the long run, for he sided with China's future when he came to bid farewell to the students in Tiananmen Square. No one, not even Deng Xiaoping himself, had ever showed such courage at such a critical juncture in the history of the CCP.

Deng Xiaoping, too, found himself in a great dilemma. Since 1979, he had been looking for a road to China's economic prosperity and status as a great power without sacrificing the fruits of the revolution. He seemed to believe that under him the CCP could lead the Chinese people into a new millennium through orderly progress, for which political stability was a precondition.[32] Consequently, he had little tolerance for political dissent, whether in or outside the party, viewing it as a dangerous destabilizing factor.

He apparently also received great pressure from the conservative camp headed by Chen Yun, who had always stayed a step behind the others and appeared correct while true heroes fumbled. Chen Yun was not openly opposed to Deng's reform, but he counseled caution and managed to get his protege, Li Peng, into the premiership following the ouster of Hu Yaobang. Without the personal charisma and undisputable authority of Mao, Deng had to yield to his opponents, sometimes at the expense of his political allies. In 1986 he sacrificed Hu Yaobang to appease his old colleagues in the CCP. In 1989, the time to sacrifice Zhao Ziyang arrived, not only because the reform had gone awry, but also because Zhao was deviating from Deng's strategy of maintaining the imaginary unity of the CCP. However, while it was relatively easy for him to drop Hu Yaobang in order to lift his reformist balloon in 1986, in 1989 it was an ordeal because he could not abandon yet another ally without curtailing the reform on which hinged the final chapter of his political career.

Within the limits of the Four Cardinal Principles, Deng could tolerate some criticism of the party, and he believed that controlled criticism of the party was good for the state and, moreover, might even help remove his rivals. However, where Mao Zedong emphasized ideological indoctrination to the populace, Deng was inclined to use economic benefits as his suasion and administrative control mechanism. His lack of imagination was compensated by a shrewd common sense and toughness of a Sichuanese. Despite the wishful effort of some China watchers to separate him from the bloodshed on June 4, 1989, he made the fatal decision to use regular troops against the demonstrators, reputedly even against the pleas of his own children.

SIGNIFICANCE OF JUNE 4, 1989

The shooting in Tiananmen of course went far beyond the will of Deng Xiaoping to revenge an insult by the youth, or even the ruthlessness of the old guards of Chinese communism. It revealed the fundamental contradiction between the heavy legacy of a revolution and China's need to join a global community. To the old guards of the Chinese revolution, a bloodbath in the capital was the only answer to the challenge from its perceived opponents. Such a fateful decision may have been a grave mistake on the part of the hardliners, nevertheless it fundamentally affected the nature of the Chinese government and its relationship with the Chinese people.

First of all, the June 4, 1989 incident prematurely testified to the emergence of a civil society, one being formed largely because of urbanization which was speeded up by the reform. It demonstrated how much China had changed since the end of the Cultural Revolution. In retrospect, one may argue that the bloodshed could only slow down China's journey toward a politically plural society, that it was impossible to totally reverse the process of political decentralization because urbanization, industrialization, and the development of the commercial economy had corroded the relative cohesion of the official ideology and party organization of the period before the Cultural Revolution.

In the history of modern China, popular protest seemed most likely to start in the cities, with their concentration of industrial and educated population. In the decade before 1989, the number of China's city dwellers jumped over 200 percent from 172 million to 541 million. In 1989, nearly 50 percent of the country's 1.1 billion people lived in cities and townships. Although only 201 million of these people were registered as urban, clearly China was no longer a nation of peasants. As the reform progressed, a growing number of migrant workers left the countryside for the cities in search for seasonal or even semi-permanent jobs. This demographic trend exposed more Chinese people, and especially the younger generation to the lure of modern amenities and the assault of new ideas. The population flow proved to be an administrative headache for the Chinese government in terms of housing, food services, and public security.

In the cities, a civil society was emerging, characterized by a vague sense of self-identity. Social groupings such as the rusticated youth of the 1970s, veterans of the Sino-Vietnam War of 1979, and teachers and college professors began to identify with one another more than ever before. While veterans held scattered demonstrations for employment, the rusticated youth petitioned for the right to return to the cities, and teachers had their feelings heard through various channels, especially the news media. Work units, too, began to develop a sense of common interest against the policy of the state in matters such as wages and salaries. The "democratic parties," whose wills were pitifully raped by the CCP during the Maoist era, revived their grass-roots organization under the renewed united front policy of the post–Mao regime and became centers of gravitation, especially among the intellectuals. Even soccer fans association in some big cities demonstrated tremendous potential. There was little coordination among the groupings, and their autonomy was both limited and fragile because of the stultifying power the CCP. Nevertheless, such new matrices of power were forming.[33]

Years of openness to the outside world and an influx of information also heightened the political consciousness of the urban population and fostered the popular desire for participation. In addition, the contradiction between concepts such as the Four Cardinal Principles and *dangzheng fenkai* (separation of party and government), or between the new authoritarianism and political realities only added simultaneously to the people's expectation and frustrations.

It was no accident that the tragic showdown should have happened in Beijing. The city was not only the nation's political nerve center, it was also a city of culture. With the mammoth bureaucracy of the CCP and its administration, 67 universities and colleges, and over 250 research institutes, the population of Beijing is undoubtedly one of the best educated in the world.

At the same time, the people in Beijing were also the most politically conscious in China. The high self-esteem of Beijing's residents could be easily called into action in a critical year like 1989, which marked several anniversaries: the seventieth anniversary of the May 4 Movement, the fortieth birthday of the People's Republic, and the bicentennial of the French Revolution. This coincidence of historically meaningful events helped intensify the already heavily charged political atmosphere in the Chinese capital.

The most peculiar—and most important—element of the 1989 Tiananmen incident was the fact that it involved groups in addition to college students and intellectuals. Liaison was established between colleges and high schools, factories, stores, and villages. Students from Beijing were seen in Nanjing, Shanghai, Wuhan, Xian, and Changsha, while students from Tianjin, Hefei, Harbin, and Hangzhou added to the number of demonstrators in Tiananmen Square.[34] For the government, the most frightening thing was the birth of a independent workers' movement during the standoff. Workers in Beijing stood on the sideline for weeks and then joined the cry for political changes. Despite the government's effort to segregate them from the students, in late May, workers in Beijing organized their autonomous union. In the "People's Decree" issued on May 29, 1989, the Beijing Workers' Autonomous Union expressed its support of the students while condemning the government. The union decried the official corruption and the leadership's inability to eradicate the evil. Especially daring was its demand for the removal of Deng Xiaoping.[35] The government arrested the union leaders, but the remaining hardliners came to camp in Tiananmen Square. During the standoff, thousands of workers from Beijing's large enterprises, such as the Yanshan Petrochemical Corporation and Capital Steel Corporation, as well as employees of numerous government departments, showed up in Tiananmen Square under their own banners.

Small independent businessmen in the city, the *getihu*, demonstrated amazing enthusiasm in the demonstration. Their spontaneously organized "Flying Tigers" provided a much-needed liaison between otherwise unrelated groups and contributed to the remarkable coordination of the demonstrators. Living under the thumbs of government officials and subject to official abuse and exaction, the *getihu* in China had not grown into a self-conscious class. Without any political agenda, they nevertheless saw in the demonstration an opportunity for expressing their grievances.[36] The Stone Company, headed by Wan Runnan, proved a big sponsor for students in Tiananmen Square, providing food and other supplies that ranged from tents to cellular telephones. The scale of defiance was unprecedented in the history of the People's Republic.[37] Thus, the movement became a showcase for an emerging civil society awakening to its power and rights, even in the limited political space allowed by the constitution of the People's Republic.

In retrospect, the 1989 democratic movement stood little chance of success. For one thing, no student movement had ever succeeded in changing a

Chinese government. To move the Chinese government, students had to ally the workers who generally did not share their demands for democracy and were more interested in curbing inflation and official corruption. The students did not—and perhaps could not—adequately identify with the workers. Rather, their action resulted from disillusionment and an outburst of emotions against the government. In a rapidly escalating situation, emotions often prevailed over reason. Moral righteousness was often accompanied by youthful exhibitionism. Most of them, with no knowledge of the CCP's history, saw the martial law as a game or a sheer bluff. Without access to the power center, demonstrating became the students' only tactic. In front of regular troops, however, they were no more than sitting ducks.

At the same time, the student leaders obviously did not possess the skill needed to achieve their political goals. In the critical days before June 4, they lost control of their followers. The majority of the demonstrators recognized neither the authority of the government nor that of their own leaders when the latter would not follow their radical demands. Some of the leaders who emerged in the second half of May thus gambled with the lives of their followers, leading the movement to a bloody showdown.[38]

Moreover, the demonstration did not strengthen the position of the reformers in the CCP, but rather reduced the room to maneuver for people like Zhao Ziyang. Throughout the standoff, no coordination was established between the students and reformers in the CCP and the government. Apparently, the student leaders were resolved to maintain their image of political innocence and therefore refused to be used by any force in the political establishment. At the same time, tight discipline in the CCP deterred Zhao Ziyang from actions that might lead to the establishment of a second center of power, however short-lived it might have been. In retrospect, one may doubt the feasibility of a student-reformer coalition. Thus, the student leaders maneuvered dangerously against the seasoned old men in Zhongnanhai toward a no-win fight. While emotions reigned, no compromise seemed proper. It was said that Deng Pufang, Deng Xiaoping's eldest son, tried to get in touch with the student leaders, but to no avail. Deng Nan, Deng Xiaoping's older daughter, went to Beida, but no one could make a deal with her.[39]

The democracy movement of 1989 failed as well because of the gap between the city and the countryside. After all, political progress in China since the late 1970s had been very uneven. While the city agitated for political reform, the rural population, content with its newly gained moderate prosperity, showed little interest in the drama in Tiananmen Square. In fact, thousands of farmers in the suburbs of Beijing were shown on Central China TV in a counterdemonstration orchestrated by the government. Elsewhere in China, farmers demonstrated the same apathy toward the demands of the intelligentsia. This of course does not mean that China's countryside had become a paradise on earth. In fact, there were complaints against official extortion and abuses in the countryside. In general, however, the farmers did not share the anxiety and frustration of the urban population. With the vast sea of rural population still impassive about political reform, it is legitimate to ask whether China had developed the social conditions conducive to political democracy.

As far as we are concerned, the incident of June 4, 1989 went far beyond the cries in Tiananmen Square and the victory of the old guards in the CCP. It was surely one of the greatest landmarks in the history of modern China. The incident proved that the Communist Party was no longer monolithic, although Deng Xiaoping and his hard-line allies won the confrontation through their control of the PLA. The chaos during the Tiananmen incident exposed once again the crumbling unity of the CCP. The behavior of thousands of government officials during the standoff only demonstrated the ruling party's susceptibility to new ideas and public sentiment.

The younger cadres were extremely receptive to the needs of the people and sympathetic with the students. Students at the People's University of China, many of whom had strong ties with the establishment, participated in the demonstration. As "party stalwarts," they were demonstrating their desire to rid the party of its chronic ailments although they were well aware that it could not be cured in a matter of days, weeks, or even months. To them, China in 1989 was undergoing another May 4th which was aimed as much at achieving political democratization as at promoting economic prosperity.[40]

The performance of Chinese press during the standoff testified to the fundamental schizophrenia of the political establishment. The press corps had enjoyed great prestige in the Communist Party whose success hinged largely on propaganda. For decades, the press remained the party's handy tool of political control. Yet self-esteem and professionalism of the press corps, which was generally better educated than the rest of the ruling elite, produced some of China's most vocal dissenters, such as Liu Binyan and Wang Ruoshui.[41]

One of the most telling facts was the rebellion of *People's Daily*. Defying the will of the old guards, reporters for the paper followed the standoff closely and empathized with the demonstrators, either directly or indirectly. In a tragic moment for the People's Republic, the organ of the ruling party sided with the people in the face of a certain purge. Nearly 600 people, or one-third of the paper's staff, showed support in various forms. Sixty percent were division-level officials.[42] The performance of the Chinese media in the 1989 crisis was a good indicator to the impasse of China's political reform and the growing professionalism among China's news corps.

Obviously, the show of popular will and the brutal denouement in Tiananmen only dealt another deadly blow to the ideology of the CCP. It demonstrated, among other things, that political orthodoxy had become totally irrelevant for the majority of the Chinese people. Without the moral authority, the party's legitimacy now hung almost exclusively on power and coercion. The Tiananmen incident of 1989 itself showed very well the difficulty for a revolutionary ideology to survive in what Deng Xiaoping call the "great international political climate" and the "small domestic political climate."[43]

By putting down demonstrators in Beijing and other Chinese cities, the regime weathered the stormiest crisis in its history. The apparent unity of the ruling party was restored, but the fundamental question remained: how could the top leadership maintain and reinforce unity when the ideological motor ceased to produce the necessary energy? The communist ideology as a value system was doomed simply because its essence ran counter to an emerging culture brought about by economic reforms. Even if the CCP succeeded in harnessing the monster of market, it would be impossible for it to keep its ideology uncontaminated. In fact, the market economy had an enormously corroding effect on the moral fiber of the CCP, and the party as a whole proved quite susceptible.

The 1989 crisis once again showed the importance of the PLA. When the government was in a total disarray in Beijing, Deng not only deployed 200,000 troops in and around Beijing, he also flew to Wuhan in central China to establish a new power center, with the military claiming allegiance to him. Like Mao Zedong, Deng knew well the importance of the military. His retention of the chairmanship of the CCP Central Military Commission was no accident. In a time of crisis when even the armed police proved unable to put down the riot, only the handy and lethal field army remained in the arsenal of Chinese communism's old guards.

By using naked force against the people's demonstration, the Beijing government broke two major precepts upon which rested its legitimacy. First, it shattered the myth that it was a government for the Chinese people, which the CCP had worked hard to establish among its own members and the Chinese people. Second, it violated the Confucian conception of a benevolent rule. After the Tiananmen shooting, it could no longer lay claim to the moral authority that belongs to a good ruler. Through the bloodletting in Tiananmen, the ruling party further alienated the Chinese people, and especially the educated segment of the population. Whatever the CCP and Chinese government did in the future would be influenced by the traumatic effects of the massacre. With an ideology nearing total bankruptcy, the Chinese government quickly moved toward a type of authoritarianism common in the Third World countries. In other words, although not announcing the failure of Marxism-Leninism-Mao Zedong Thought, the party increasingly came to depend on the use of the police force and the military for keeping the peace.

As had happened time and again in China's modern history, in 1989 the old leaders strangled the aspirations of the young idealists. Veterans of the Long March proved unwilling to yield to the new forces for change. Resolved to preserve what was left of the Chinese Communist movement, Deng Xiaoping, Chen Yun, Li Xiannian, Peng Zhen, Deng Yinchao and Yang Shangkun agreed that there was no other alternative. After the Tiananmen incident, the octogenarians in Beijing continually intimidated their younger colleagues to keep them in line.

The net result was not, however, totally favorable to those. For one thing, this was a Pyrrhic victory which cost Deng Xiaoping his political capital. Second, the old guards' days were numbered. Deng Xiaoping had to retire even though he was still dissatisfied with the Jiang Zemin-Li Peng axis. An even more dangerous factor was the illegality of the old men's decisions first to oust Hu Yaobang, and then to remove Zhao Ziyang. These decisions could be easily overturned at a party congress and there was no guarantee that the next generation of Chinese leaders would carry the cross for Deng Xiaoping. As soon as the government encounters trouble, Deng Xiaoping is likely to be sacrificed, either by the reformers or by hard-line Maoists.

Despite the sweeping victory of the military crackdown, any conservative restoration faced an insurmountable obstacles, chief of which was the public sentiment which had become impervious to political orthodoxy. It was simply impossible to wash away the memories of over 6 million Beijing residents. Ideologues such as Deng Liqun, Yuan Mu, and Gao Di were active for a short time. But they soon proved to be a political liability for Deng as they were unpopular among the people, especially the educated. Moreover, these conservatives had been critical of Deng Xiaoping's reform since the early 1980s and had no interest in continuous openness. Deng's alliance with them came out of sheer political expediency. The new core of the leadership centered on Jiang Zeming, a bland technocrat and former mayor of Shanghai, was a strange mixture of individuals. However, like its predecessors, the new leadership showed a high degree of instability and discord.

In a few years, the old guards of the Chinese revolution will die off, leaving a heavy legacy for their successors. For the new generation of Chinese leaders, there will be two alternatives. The first is to continue the policy of tight control within the nation along with opening to the outside (*neijin waisong*) and to put down any popular protest, especially a protest bearing upon the June 4 Tiananmen incident, before it can gain momentum.[44] This will prove extremely difficult. The reversal of the verdict on the April 5 Incident of 1976 is a precedent. The other, and perhaps more sensible policy is to denounce the massacre, in the manner of the Li Denghui administration with the April 22th Incident of 1947 in Taiwan. That will free the party from the infamy of Tiananmen, and the Chinese mainlanders are not likely to wait forty-odd years for this to come about. However, given the intricacy of Chinese politics and the personal stakes involved, no one can foresee what chain reaction such a policy will cause. In any event, June 4, 1989 added tremendous uncertainty to any forecast of China's near future.

NOTES

1. Andrew Nathan, *China's Crisis: Dilemmas for Reform and Prospects for Democracy* (New York: Columbia University Press, 1990), p. 37.

2. Ibid.

3. *Beijing Review*, September 4–10, 1989, pp. 22–28.

4. Cheng Jieyuan, "Zhongguo nongchun gaige de wenti" (Problems with China's agricultural reforms), *Ming Bao Monthly*, August 1990, pp. 15–18.

5. See Cheng, *Behind the Tiananmen Massacre: Social, Political, and Economic Ferment in China* (Boulder, Colo.: Westview Press, 1990), pp. 58–59; Shi Xiaoming, "Weiji yishi yu Zhongguo wentixue" (Crisis consciousness and China studies), *Dushu* (Reading), April 1989, p. 41.

6. Fang Lizhi, "Will China Collapse?" in *Bringing Down the Great Wall: Writings on Science, Culture, and Democracy in China*, ed. and trans. James H. Williams (New York: W. W. Norton & Co., 1990), p. 231.

7. Ibid, pp. 236–2377.

8. Ibid, p. 232.

9. Deng Xiaoping, "On the Reform of the System of the Party and State Leadership," in *Selected Works of Deng Xiaoping, 1975–1984* (Beijing: Foreign Language Press, 1984), p. 315.

10. See Zhang Weixuan, Liu Wuyi, and Xiao Xing, eds., *Gongheguo fengyun sishi nian* (Forty eventful years of the republic), (Beijing: Political Science and Law University Press, 1989), pp. 1464–1467; Xu Luo and Luo Ning, "Political and Ideological Origins of the Crisis," in Roger V. Des Forges, Luo Ning, and Wu Yenbo, eds., *Chinese Democracy and the Crisis of 1989: Chinese and American Reflections* (Albany: State University of New York Press, 1993), pp. 98–105; Wang Xiaodong, "A Review of China's Economic Problems: The Industrial Sector," in ibid, pp. 149–160.

11. Cheng, *Behind the Tiananmen Massacre*, p. 24.

12. Xu Haibo, "Zhongguo qiye de laoshi guanxi wenti—xianzhuang, fenxi ji duice" (The employer-employee relationship in Chinese enterprises—current situation, analysis, and policy suggestions), *Renda baokan fuyin ziliao* (Xeroxed Articles in Newspapers and Periodicals by the People's University), no. 1 (January 1987): 26; Shaoguang Wang, "A Force for Change," in Forges, Luo, and Wu, eds., *Chinese Democracy*, pp. 185–6.

13. Jeanne Wilson, "Labor Policy in China: Reform and Retrogression," *Problems of Communism* 39 (Sept-Oct 1990): 58–59; Shi Yongfeng & Xiao Binchen, "Miandui shiye kunhuo de Zhongguo gongren," (Chinese workers in the face of unemployment), *Liao Wang* (Lookout), September 5, 1988, p. 22; Tong Yanyi, "Beijing: Wujing de youluu" (Beijing: Endless anxiety), *Jiushi Niandai* (Nineteen-Nineties), June 1988, pp. 35–37.

14. See Cheng Ying, "Gaige yu minsheng: zhen yige chouzi liaode" (Reform and people's livelihood: Anxiety prevails), *Nineties*, June 1988, pp. 38–41; Cheng Ying,

"Zhongnian zhishi fenzi duo zaoshi" (Middle-aged intellectuals died young) *Nineties*, April 1988, pp. 19–21.

15. Fang, "China's Despair and China's Hope," in *Bringing Down the Great Wall*, p. 256.

16. Edward Gunn, "The Rhetoric of River Elegy: From Cultural Criticism to Social Act," in Forges, Luo & Wu eds., *Chinese Democracy*, pp. 247–261.

17. According to Su Xiaokang, coauthor of the *River Elegy*, even government agencies such as the municipal Bureau of Public Security made it mandatory for their employees to watch the series in order to better understand the meaning of reform. See Su Xiaokang, "Heshang xuechao wenhua bianqian" (The *River Elegy*, student movement, and cultural transformation: Speech at the University of Kentucky), *Zhongguo zhi Chun* (China Spring), June 1991, pp. 63–65.

18. Fang, *Bringing Down the Great Wall*, p. 102.

19. Wang Luo and Yang Xiaokai, "Chinese Dissident Movement," *Zhishi Fenzi* (Chinese Intellectual), Fall 1992, pp. 26–27.

20. Wang Runsheng, "Cong shehui gongneng kan xin qimeng de deshi" (Social consequences: A balance sheet for the new enlightenment), *China Spring*, August 1991, pp. 59–61.

21. Ibid, p. 61; He Xin, "Zhongguo dangdai wenhua beiwanglu: wo de kunhuo yu youluu" (A memorandum on contemporary Chinese culture: My bewilderment and worry), *Jingjixue Zhoubao* (Economics Weekly) January 8, 1989, pp. 6–8.

22. Stuard R. Schram, "Economics in Command? Ideology and Policy since the Third Plenum, 1978–1984," *China Quarterly* 99 (September 1984): 441.

23. Zhang Guangzhao, "Shehui jinbu xuyao yanlun ziyou" (Social progress depends on the freedom of speech), *World Economy Herald*, October 3, 1988; also see Nathan, *China's Crisis*, pp. 117–8.

24. Meng Xiaoyun & Wang Chu, "Shiyi yi zhongguo renmin wei ni shongxing" (1.1 billion Chinese people bid you farewell), *Renmin Ribao* (People's Daily), April 23, 1989.

25. Wu'er Kaixi, "How Naive We Were," Peter Li, Steven Mark, and Marjorie H. Li, eds., *Culture and Politics in China: An Anatomy of Tiananmen Square* (New Brunswick, N.J.: Translation Publishers, 1991), pp. 38–39.

26. King K. Tsao, "Civil Disobedience and Dissent against the Party-State: An Eyewitness Account of the 1989 Chinese Student Movement," in Li, Mark, and Li, eds., *Culture and Politics in China*, p. 164.

27. See Liu Binyan, *Tell the World: What Happened in China and Why* (New York: Pantheon Books, 1989), pp. 122–123.

28. Editorial, "Bixu qizhi xianming di fandui dongluan" (Resolutely oppose turmoil), *People's Daily*, April 26, 1989.

29. Lee Feigon, *China Rising: The Meaning of Tiananmen* (Chicago, Ill.: Iven Dee, 1990), pp. 120–121, 127; Wu Guoguang, "The Dilemma of Participation in the

Political Reform of China, 1986–1988," in Forges, Luo and Wu eds., *Chinese Democracy*, pp. 143–145.

30. Ai Feng, "Butong pingjia yuanhe we sheng: shixi dui dangqian gaige xingshi de renshi" (What accounts for the differing assessments: Our understanding of the current state of the reform), *People's Daily*, November 25, 1988.

31. Li Peng, "Report to the Second Session of the Seventh National People's Copngress," in *Issues and Studies* 25 (April 1989): 1–4.

32. Deng Xiaoping, "Woguo fangzhen zhengce de liangge jiben dian" (Two basic points in our policies and decisions), *Deng Xiaoping Wenxuan* (Selected works of Deng Xiaoping) (Beijing: Renmin Press, 1993), 3:248–250; "Yiqie cong shehui zhuyi chuji jieduan de shiji chufa" (Base all our policies on the reality of the primary stage of socialism), in ibid, pp. 251–252.

33. Richard Madsen, "The Public Sphere, Civil society and Moral Community," *Modern China* 19 (April 1993): 183–197; Heath B. Chamberlain, "On the Search for Civil Society in China," *Modern China* 19 (April 1993): 199–213; Mark Selden, "The Social Origins and Limits of the Democratic Movement," in Forges, Luo and Wu, eds., *Chinese Democracy*, pp. 125–128. Selden nevertheless adds som equalifiers to the conceptualization. This is perhaps because he considers June 4th, 1989 a democratic movement from the very outset.

34. Chen Xitong (mayor of Beijing and a state councillor), "Report on Checking the Turmoil and Quelling the Counter-Revolutionary Rebellion [June 30, 1989, National Central Committee of the Communist Party]," in Li, Mark, and Li, eds., *Culture and Politics in China*, p. 72.

35. *Culture and Politics in China*, pp. 31–34.

36. Feigon, *China Rising*, p. 222.

37. Ibid, pp. 232, 236.

38. Yao Yongzhan, "Huigu shanghai bajiu minyun" (Reflection of the democracy movement in Shanghai, 1989), *China Spring*, June 1992, p. 11; Yao, "Lun xueyun lingxiu" (On the leaders of the student movement of 1989), *China Spring*, August 1991, pp. 56–58; Chen Yizhi, "Renlei buhui wangji-jinian liusi canan san zhounian" (The mankind will never forget: The third Anniversary of the June 4th massacre of 1989), *China Spring*, June 1992, pp. 9–10; Josephine M. T. Khu, "Student Organization in the Movement," Forges, Luo, and Wu, eds., *Chinese Democracy*, pp. 170–171; Lucien Pye, "Tiananmen and Chinese Political Culture: The Escalation of Confrontation from Moralizing to Revenge," *Asian Survey* 30 (April 1990): 331–347.

39. Jiang Zhifeng, *Wangpai chujin de Zhongnanhai qiaoju* (The bridge game without trump cards) (San Francisco, Calif.: Democratic China Books Press, 1990), p. 108.

40. Feigon, *China Rising*, pp. 131–132.

41. Michael J. Berlin, "The Performance of the Chinese Media during the Beijing Spring," in Forges, Luo and Wu, eds., *Chinese Democracy*, pp. 263–275; Frank Tan,

"The People's Daily and the Epiphany of Press Reform," in ibid, pp. 277–294; Judy Polumbaum, "'Professionalism' in China's Press Corps," in ibid, pp. 295–311.

42. Zi Yie, "Renmin Ribao Sanshiba Xiaoshi de Zhengza" (*People's Daily*: Thirty-eight hours' desperate struggle), *World Journal*, May 30, 1993; Yi Ke, "Renmin ribao de wange" (The dirge of the *People's Daily*), *China Spring*, October 1991, pp. 62–64; Li Zao, "Wu Xuechan yu remin ribao" (Wu Xuechan and the *People's Daily*), *Beijing Spring*, October 1993, pp. 54–56; Zheng Chuyuan, "Liusi zhengjing Beijing yu zhongguo dalu qiantu" (Political and economic background of the June 4th and the future of China), *Ming Bao Monthly*, June 1991, pp. 13–15.

43. Deng, "Zai jiejian shoudu jieyan budui jun yishang ganbu shi de jiang hua" (Speech during the reception for the Commanders of the armies enforcing martial law in Beijing),in *Selected Works*, 3:302.

44. Deng, "Zai jiejian shoudu jieyan budui jun yishang ganbu de jianghua" *Selected Works*, 3:307.

5

China Since the Tiananmen Crackdown

The Tiananmen crackdown signified a major setback in China's journey toward political modernization. In the West as well, it helped create a deep disillusionment among China experts. Concerned pundits lamented the abortion of China's democracy and the carnage of China's innocent youth. Indeed, what happened in the wake of Tiananmen seemed to support every pessimistic speculation about the nation's immediate future. The political development since Tiananmen, however, proves to be much more complicated and dramatic than most outsiders had anticipated. Out of chaos, a more sophisticated political equilibrium has emerged, with new patterns of interplay between the Chinese people and their government that serve to maintain a necessary, though fragile, truce. For better or for worse, China has survived the trauma of Tiananmen, and its economy is now growing with a vengeance under an authoritarian government.

The tragedy of 1989 revealed, among other things, the enormous difficulty for a ruling party with a revolutionary history to embark on a course of economic liberalization. It also exposed the vulnerability of Deng Xiaoping's reformist program which, while it brought prosperity into some segments of Chinese society, had engendered tremendous strains and a sense of insecurity in others. Besides, if the state throughout China's history always swings back and forth between the *wen* (civility) and *wu* (violence), the use of naked force in June 1989 reinforced the *wu* nature of the post–Mao regime.

For its own survival, the government had not only to justify the use of force, however awkward its apology, but also to strengthen and institutionalize its instruments of repression, especially the police force, as its principal means to maintain social stability. At the same time, it had also to live up, at least nominally, to both international norms and Chinese precepts about good government. Under pressure from both within and without, the Chinese government developed policies that combined tradition with the paraphernalia of a modern authoritarian state.

POLITICAL READJUSTMENT

The use of force helped the regime survive a major crisis, but it by no means solved the fundamental problems in the political system. In some respects, these problems became even more urgent. First of all, the government needed to restore order in the aftermath of Tiananmen. This was not easy, even after the soldiers had subjugated the capital. Scattered resistance continued for weeks after June 4 and many top organizers of the demonstration went into hiding. The task was complicated by confusion in the police force and the general uncooperative attitude on the part of the urban residents. Second, given the trauma of Tiananmen, it was imperative to stop the downturn in the economy which, while contributing to the popular revolt in May and June, was likely to accelerate due to popular antipathy and Western economic sanctions. Third, there was the almost impossible job of restoring the government's reformist image by justifying the bloodshed. Because of the presence of the Western news corps in Beijing during the crisis, the government could do virtually nothing to alter world opinion. To people at home, the government had to explain why as many as 20 million citizens had taken to the streets and why the crisis could not have been solved in a less brutal manner. Above all, the post-Tiananmen Chinese leadership had to regroup the government and the ruling party to pull them out of utter confusion.

As had happened after every major crisis in CCP's history, the Tiananmen incident resulted in another major reshuffling at the top of the party and the government. Zhao Ziyang was put under house arrest and his adherents encountered near-total liquidation. Of the 130 members of the Institute for the Reform of the Economic System (*jingji Tizhi Gaige Yanjiu suo*), Zhao's think tank, more than 20, including the economist Yan Jiaqi, fled the country, and 8 of them were arrested, including Bao Tong, Zhao's right-hand. Some prominent officials who had been openly sympathetic with the students likewise fell, including Wang Meng, Minister of Cultural Affairs,[1] Zhu Houze, Minister of Propaganda of the Central Committee of the CCP, Wang Fang, Minister of Public Security, and Liang Xiang, the reformist governor of Hainan province.[2] Key departments of the government, especially organs of propaganda such as the *People's Daily*, CCTV, and Radio Beijing were thoroughly purged.[3] Since major organs of the party such as the *People's Daily* and CCTV expressed sympathy toward the demonstrators, they were taken over by either military or political appointees of the old guards. Gao Di, an ideologue known for his ultra-leftist views, became editor-in-chief of the *People's Daily*. He Jingzhi, a notorious "*gede*" (adulation) poet, replaced Wang Meng as the Minister of

Cultural Affairs.[4] To assert its proletarian character, the CCP altered its policy of absorbing capitalists into its ranks, a reversal that indicates the profound contradiction between a communist regime and a market economy.

All in all, conservatives were the immediate beneficiaries of the purge. However, Deng Xiaoping's decisive role in the crackdown prevented them from attaining a total victory. After the removal of Zhao Ziyang, Deng continued to keep some allies as a check on the power of Chen Yun and Li Peng. Deng Xiaoping's most noticeable move was to promote Jiang Zemin, mayor of Shanghai, to the post of the general secretary of the CCP and Li Ruihuan, mayor of Tianjin, to the capital to handle the party's propaganda. The transitional leadership after Tiananmen was thus a product of compromise. Li Peng and Yao Yilin were Chen Yun's proteges, Li Ruihuan and Yang Shangkun were Deng's allies, and Jiang Zemin, Song Ping, and Qiao Shi were, by and large, neutral. Jiang Zemin was chosen by Deng Xiaoping because his of success in handling the student demonstrations in Shanghai in 1989 and his apparent lack of ambition.[5] He was also a person who would not antagonize hard-liners in the party. The problem with Jiang was his and indecision and lukewarm interest in continuing economic reform. Without much of a power base in Beijing, Jiang tried, by necessity, to be friendly to both Deng's allies and his rivals.

A very ironic, but remarkable, move by Deng Xiaoping after the Tiananmen crackdown was the appointment of Li Ruihuan as the party's propaganda chief. Despite his lack of formal education, Li Ruihuan proved to be an expert in carrot-and-stick tactics. During the 1989 crisis, he avoided bloodshed in Tianjin as the mayor of that city by permitting demonstrations within certain limits. In Tianjin he distinguished himself as a reformer by improving the livelihood of the people and enjoyed some popularity among the educated for his moderate view on literature and art. On the other hand, he was blunt enough to assert the determination of the power center to use force to deal with any future dissent. He became the spokesman of the new regime in cultural affairs and a tool with which to impose a climate of peace and harmony (*xianghe*).

Resorting to force to deal with civilians was not new to the Chinese government. During the Cultural Revolution, regular forces were used to put down rebels in provinces such as Qinghai and Yunnan. In the 1980s, the government showed the same determination in cracking down the "separatist movement" in Lhasa, Tibet. But atrocities in the capital of the People's Republic proved too great a political liability for the government in the long run. The horrendous cost of the suppression convinced the government that it needed a greater deterrent power to preclude future turmoil. Deng Xiaoping, Jiang Zemin, and other leaders claimed to have learned a lesson from June 4, 1989 and vowed to be better prepared for future disorder. Sure enough, in the wake of Tiananmen, the government reinforced its police force in the major cities, especially Beijing.[6] Political indoctrination resumed in the police department with a focus on the danger of "peaceful transformation." Officers who had appeared soft in 1989 were punished or censured.[7] Quickly motorized, the urban police also acquired anti-riot weapons including imported tear gas and received intensive anti-riot training. Video cameras were installed at major intersections in Beijing to detect unusual activities by pedestrians. On the anniversaries of June 4, armed police forces patrolled Beijing's streets and college campuses. Beida and Tiananmen were put under especially tight control. The strategy of damping out any sparks before they could cause a fire worked reasonably well. Although students at Beida remained defiant, no serious incidents ever occurred around June 4 between 1990 and 1994.

The Tiananmen incidnet of 1989 undoubtedly boosted the position of the PLA in the government. The crucial role of the PLA in putting down the popular rebellion gave military leaders more chips in their bargain with the civilian leaders. In 1990, China's military budget increased by 15.2 percent, which was unique in the general international atmosphere.[8] The loyalty of the PLA, though it had passed the test of the 1989 crisis, had to be reasserted. At the end of 1989, the Central Military Commission endorsed a document concerning political work in the military which called for tighter ideological control and political indoctrination among the rank-and-file of the PLA. Organs of the party such as *Qiushi* attacked the tendency of de-politicization of the military prior to June 4, 1989, as a dangerous step toward undermining the proletarian dictatorship.[9]

In the months following Tiananmen, the Chinese government pursued a policy of "swift arrest, heavy sentence" (*kuaibu zhongshen*). In a report to the central committee of the CCP and the state council, the Beijing municipal government recommended the close cooperation of the procuratorate, the court, and the bureau of public security to carry out "swift arrest, immediate trial, and instantaneous sentence" of the leading rioters. It proposed death penalty for those who "deserved" it and mass meetings at which to announce such sentences in order to "educate and mobilize the masses and to deter future perpetrators."[10]

The ruthlessness of the crackdown exceeded that of the political campaigns of the 1950s, whose primary target had been the intellectuals, rather than ordinary citizens.[11] Thousands of individuals were rounded up, interrogated, prosecuted, and given harsh penalties including capital punishment. In the very spirit of community surveillance of *Bao-Jia*,[12] citizens were told to turn in their relatives who were on the government's list, for knowing a crime but not reporting was a crime as well. In a climate of terror, antigovernment speech became a serious offence. A case in point is the story of Xiao Bin, who received a ten-year prison sentence for condemning the government before a Western television camera. The harshest penalty, however, was noticeably meted out, not to student leaders, but to old dissidents such as Wang Juntao and Chen Ziming, Zhao's top advisors, and especially, peasants, workers, and jobless people whose activities violated criminal laws. Obviously the students still enjoyed traditional immunity to heavy penalty and the government was reluctant to widen the wounds of Tiananmen.[13] In fact, the government carried out a calculated policy of "killing the chicken to scare the monkeys."

It is worth noting, however, that the reprisal was much less severe than many observers, in China and abroad, had expected. In January 1990, martial law was lifted in Beijing, eight months after the crackdown. At the same time, the government released 573 people who had been jailed for participation in the demonstration. In May, the Ministry of Public Security freed 221 people, including 6 well-known intellectuals: Li Honglin, Cao Siyuan, Dai Qing, Yang Baikui, Li Nanyou, and Zhou Duo. In June, the government announced that it had freed 860 people altogether, reducing the number still in confinement to 355. Between June and December 1990, the government released Wang Ruowang, a leading dissident writer, Wen Yuankai, a famous scholar-reformer, and Ye Wenfu, a bold poet and social critic. Most noticeably, Beijing allowed Fang Lizhi and his wife to leave the U.S. embassy in Beijing, where they had sought asylum to come to the United States for "medical treatment." Student leaders received relatively light penalties. Wang Dan, the leader of the Beida students, received only four years in prison. Some of his comrades were set free even without prosecution on the grounds that they were "penitent" about their crimes. Liu Xiaobo, China's famous literary critic and a leading hunger striker in Tiananmen Square, was released for "rewardable behavior." All this looked farcical in light of the thundering propaganda that immediately followed June 4. The decision reflected an urgent need to return to the normalcy of reform, even though the acquittal was tantamount to acknowledging the government's own mistake in 1989.

The rather lenient attitude toward college students and intellectuals sharply contrasted with the Chinese government's policy toward political opposition in the past. In the 1960s and 1970s, the heads of so-called counterrevolutionary organizations generally received the death penalty. The reasons for such leniency were manifold. First of all, the demonstration of 1989, despite the tragic loss of lives and property, was peaceful. Because of this, prosecution of student leaders would only further deepen the wounds that the government was anxious to heal. Pressure from the international community, especially sanctions from the Western nations, took a toll. June 4 turned the Beijing regime into an international pariah while economic sanctions immediately jeopardized China's reform and continued openness.[14] Mao Zedong, with his puritanical vision of China, would have totally ignored the West's limited cold war against China. Deng Xiaoping could not afford to do so although he briefly defied the angry international community.[15] However, by ordering the shooting in Tiananmen, he had overspent the political capital he had accumulated since 1979, and he would be the biggest loser of all if he allowed the hard-liners to have their way on all matters.

Inside the party, there was also the voice of caution since it did not take much wisdom to realize the debilitating effect of Tiananmen. Qiao Shi, a member of the Standing Committee of the Politburo in charge of legal affairs counseled clemency toward students and intellectuals. Apparently, he did not want to bear the cross for Deng Xiaoping. Even Chen Yun, Deng Xiaoping's major rival in the party hierarchy, criticized the government's rashness in dealing with June 4, 1989 crisis. Harsh penalties would, of course, help deter antigovernment activities, but it would also create further hostility among China's educated people. For the CCP, political stability was the foremost concern in order toensure survival and economic growth. Conscious of the damage of the June 4, the party was anxious to reestablish its credibility. Thus in 1990 and 1991, "harmony" (*xianghe*) became the buzzword for government officials and government-controlled media, with a view to diffusing, if not erasing, people's memory of the Tiananmen shooting.[16]

In fact, what the government did during and after Tiananmen ran counter to the traditional Chinese conception about the *wangdao* (the king's way), an authority that combined moral suasion and exemplary deeds. The crackdown of 1989 was so unpopular that the new leadership would rather, paradoxically, minimize the effect of the incident while talking about the real danger of subversive activities. On the one hand, it had to reaffirm the party's policy of continuing openness while denouncing the so-called bourgeois liberalization.[17] On the other, Li Ruihuan, who was entrusted with the difficult job to work in cultural affairs, would throw olive twigs to the intellectuals at various occasions.[18]

To a party which rode on the dream of the youth to power, it was painful to declare college campuses to be critical "disaster-stricken areas." The government reimposed measures of thought control such as political studies in all institutions of higher education. For the first time in the history of the People's Republic, plain-clothed police patrolled campuses in Beijing on a regular basis to prevent antigovernment activities. For the hard-liners, China's higher education since the beginning of the reform was a total failure for it produced nothing but some anti-party, anti-socialist elements. The government attributed the students' unruly behavior to their teachers' misleading instruction as well as the intrusion of Western values. Professors were required to make self-criticism and report what they had done during the riots, a heavy-handed policy reminiscent of the inquisition during the Cultural Revolution. The student leaders had to confess their "criminal activities" in order to maintain their eligibility or they would be expelled from school.[19] Freshmen of Beida and Qinghua University were required to receive a one-year military training, a measure designed to segregate the freshmen from the "contaminated" upper classes which were undergoing "ideological rectification."

Under the slogan of "cleaning up the economic environment" and "readjusting economic order," the government made some gestures in dealing with the *guandao*. The party reasserted its discipline and vowed to deal with corruption harshly. Between the Thirteenth and the Fourteenth Congresses, the disciplinary department of the CCP dealt with 874,690 cases of corruption involving 733,543 members, of whom 154,289 were expelled from the party. A total of 127 high-ranking officials received various forms of punishment; 15 of them lost their membership.[20]

Behind the smoke screen of "readjustment" conservatives in Beijing intensified their propaganda in order to reinforce their great, if short-lived, victory. Conservatives such as Deng Liqun, who reemerged in the blood of Tiananmen, revived fundamentalist Maoism with a view to negating the Dengist reform. In their eagerness to preserve the Maoist revolution, they even tried to reverse the verdict on the Cultural Revolution and the Great Leap Forward. Once again they invoked the dichotomy between capitalism and socialism and heightened the rhetoric against subversive activities especially by international capitalism. To people who feared change and the unpredictable future, the ten years of openness had produced indeed enough social and political evils to justify a return to Mao's puritanical China.

Class struggle, a term that had long been discredited, once again figured prominently in editorials and speeches of government officials. Hard-liners talked very loudly about subversive activities by enemies of the government. Party members and government officials were required to give unreserved support to the central committee which was now headed by Jiang Zemin. Government employees were required to study Deng Xiaoping's speeches as oracles in the same fashion as they had studied Mao's works in the 1960s and 1970s. Political cadres came out of their long hibernation, trying to regain their lost ideological position. Fear was used effectively to deter further dissention in the party. The Ministry of Propaganda put together a documentary film for the party's rank and file to show them the disastrous consequences of an anti-communist rebellion.

Negative campaigns and punitive measures alone, however, could not restore the morale of the much-dispirited party. Thus, the official organs launched a campaign to rebuild the party's vitality by establishing positive examples. In the spring of 1990, the government revoked the ghost of Lei Feng, a PLA soldier who embodied both communist populism and discipline. To mend the broken image of the party and the army, some "Living Lei Fengs" were found out and honored.[21] The sad truth about the campaign was that few, if any, party or government officials could identify with these saint-like individuals. China had long ago passed the puritanical age of the Communist revolution and the party had become too sophisticated and self-seeking to emulate a "selfless" soldier. Naturally, the anachronistic campaign failed to take off in spite of vigorous promotion by party celebrities and the news media. if any thing, it indicated the retrogressive thinking and helplessness of the party machine. The futility of the post-Tiananmen brainwashing campaign was well-demonstrated by the fact that the government soon changed the tone from punitive to conciliatory and pick up the old concept of multi-party coalition under the CCP's leadership while warning against any anti-government agitation.[22]

A DUBIOUS BATTLE

Renewed political repression did silence the agitation for political reform and criticism of the government in public. Nontheless, the government was unable to regain the people's confidence and hence could not achieve total control. A significant indicator of the limits of state power after June 4 was the fact that despite the government's strenuous effort to arrest all prominent leaders, a significant number, including Chai Lin and Urkaixi, fled the country via an underground railway, apparently with the assistance of many people, some fairly high in the power structure. Even more outrageous to the government was the public defiance during the roundup campaign. People called the military and police stations from unidentified locations, reporting their involvement in the demonstration. While mocking the government leaders, their phone calls were also intended to jam the hot lines so that real informers could not get through.[23] In their own work units, people learned to keep silent or falsify stories to protect themselves and each other. Such defiance had never before occurred in the history of the people's republic. An authoritarian government may have enough power to knock out centers of open opposition outside the political establishment, but it canot control the thought of the populace as effectively as a totalitarian regime. In the face of public antipathy, the government cpromptly alled off campaign to avoid further alienating the people.

Obviously the people not only developed immunity to party propaganda, they also learned to express their feelings against the government in unpunishable ways.[24] For instance, on July 1, the seventieth anniversary of the CCP, while one thousand youths took the oath to join the CCP before the Monument to the People's Heroes, Beijing's streets were conspicuously dotted with people wearing T-shirts on which a slogan read: "I'm not feeling well. Leave Me alone [fan zhao ne, bie li wo]." The protest and crackdown on such T-shirts made the government look stupid and impotent. Victims of persecution, such as Xue Fei and Du Xian, broadcasters of the CCTV who showed up on the screen in black clothes on June 4, 1989, became popular heroes instead of public enemies as would have been the case during the Maoist era.[25] In 1991, the authority estimated that in Beijing alone, there were at least 60 underground organizations in active operation.[26] Even at the *People's Daily* where purges surpassed those of 1957 and the Cultural Revolution of 1966–1976, people refused to cooperate with the newly appointed leadership.[27] The moral courage demonstrated by the staff of the *People's Daily* was a good barometer of public sentiment. Many party members and government officials followed their conscience instead of the Central Committee's directives, even at the risk of their political career.

The government's public approval rate hit an all-time low. While the years of economic reform had created a thaw in which limited free speech was possible, Tiananmen of 1989 and the ensuing political backlash further stripped the ruling party of its aura. The Chinese people's passive disobedience further exposed the government's waning authority. Public opinion influenced the rank and file of the ruling party and different opinions in the party found their way to the top, like an invisible hand shaping the decision-making process among the leaders.[28]

Given the shock, confusion, and smoldering hatred of the people in Beijing and other major cities, coupled with pressure from outside the country, stability understandably became the predominant concern of the new leadership. In economy, the pace of reform was slowed for fear of runaway inflation while planned economy was reemphasized. Chen Yun and Li Peng would not openly oppose economic reform. Instead, they wanted to alter its direction toward the left. Wu Shuqing, the newly appointed president of Beida, discussed the congenital weaknesses of the market economy in the *People's Daily*, echoing Li Peng and Chen Yun's policy of returning to the pre-reform cage economy, i.e., an economy following central planning. The government also found it necessary to bring inflation under control in order to appease the embittered populace.[29]

Stringent measures from Beijing, however, failed to yield desired results. Rather, between 1989 and 1992, China underwent the most stagnant period since the end of the Cultural Revolution. The Chinese people's political apathy and the party's inability to carve out a new course of action only threw China's economic reform further into the doldrums. In 1989, 2.4 million collective and private enterprises were forced to shut down, primarily because of onerous taxes. In Beijing, taxes on the *getihu* increased as much as tenfold, leading people to believe that the raw deal was a hidden reprisal for the *getihu*'s active role during the Tiananmen standoff. Millions of workers lost their jobs.[30] The new leadership, under the slogan of rectification and readjustment (*zhili zhengdun*), soft-peddled China's economic reform, trying to stop the downturn of the industrial sector by intervening heavily in the large state-owned enterprises. To reduce popular unrest caused by economic hardship, the government had to resort to a deficit economy, using pay raise and subsidies in state-own industry.[31]

In 1990, Beijing claimed progress such as continuous industrial growth, stable prices, and a profitable foreign trade. In reality, however, low productivity and a sluggish market had brought many state-owned enterprises to the brink of financial ruin. Experts warned of a vicious cycle of between growth and recession. The government had to provide large amounts of money and a favorable toward state-owned industry to avoid this.[32] As a result, younger conservatives in the CCP, such as Chen Yuan, the son of Chen Yun, called for a further return to the planned economy model to weaken economic regionalism, or the so-called dukedom economy (*zhuhou jingji*) and to close the gap between the rich and poor provinces.[33]

The bottom line of the issue was the survival of the regime. The dissolution of the Soviet Union and the collapse of communist regimes in the East European countries sent shock waves eastward. In Beijing, government organs gave carefully tailored coverage to the political transformation in those countries while vowing to resist "peaceful transformation" by the capitalist West. The Central Committee of the CCP laid out its reaction in "five adherences" and "five againsts," i.e., adhere to the leadership of the CCP, against the multi-party system; adhere to the party's control of the military, against the military's participation in politics; adhere the people's democratic dictatorship, against the parliamentary system; adhere to socialism over social democracy; adhere to an economic system based on public ownership versus privatization. The *People's Daily* called upon the party to remain confident in the eventual triumph of socialism.[34] At the same time, the dissolution the Union of the Soviet Socialist Republics must have dashed the hope of the "Soviet Faction" in the CCP and sent a strong message to many members of the political establishment to keep a distance from the hard-liners.[35]

By 1992, it became apparent that a return to the orthodox Marxism and cage economy was not a remedy for the ailing party. Deng Xiaoping had waited long enough for his opponents to expose their reactionary philosophy. If both sides were interested in preserving the fruits of the Communist revolution, they nevertheless differed significantly on how to do it. Such difference was suggested by the editorial in *People's Daily* on July 1, 1991:

Our party is facing a severe test, that is, whether we can preserve our ideological purity in a time of openness and reform when commercial economy developed and whether we can build a great wall of steel against the peaceful transformation by hostile powers both at home and abroad. This is also an important topic in our organizational building.[36]

To what extent such point of view represented Deng Xiaoping's thought is open to question.

Deng began to emphatically reiterate his pragmatic philosophy in 1990. At one occasion, he said, "The only way we measure our policy and its execution is to find out whether they help enhance productivity."[37] He and his followers refused to see the basic incompatibility between socialism and a market economy. The appointment in 1992 of Zhou Jiahua and Zhu Rongji, both technocrats, as vice premiers was obviously Deng's victory. At the same time, his decision also largely reflected the irreversibility of China's economic reform.

The result of the tug-of-war between rival factions in Beijing was indecisive and often contradictory voices from the top of the party and the government. For example, when Li Peng blamed the recalcitrant students for the June 4, 1989, crisis, Li Ruihuan, the carpenter-turned-minister, would say that the party, on the other hand, also had an undeniable responsibility in the event. When hard-liners emphasized stability to oppose necessary changes, the party chief of Heilongjiang province, Sun Benli would say: "We cannot allow stability to become a shackle on us. If so, thought emancipation and innovativeness would be weakened and the much needed reform would be shunned." The most well-known political balloon of the reformers was an editorial in the *Sichaun Daily* entitled, "Remain Focused on Economic Growth" which repeated Deng Xiaoping's idea and suggested quite threateningly, that certain forces in the party hierarchy were, in effect, sabotaging the economic reform.[38]

Such confusion and uncertainty in the party was well demonstrated by the treatment of Zhao Ziyang. The hard-liners tried to indict the ousted secretary general for alleged crimes and an investigation was carried out to incriminate him. Deng Xiaoping and the other reformers were reticent. For one thing, Zhao had been Deng's right arm throughout the early 1980s and he could not totally discredit Zhao without jeopardizing his own reputation. While Deng gladly accepted the title of the "chief architect" of China's reform, he found it necessary to call Zhao the "chief engineer." Besides, under the watchful eyes of the Chinese people and the world community, the trial of Zhao Ziyang would only help defame an already troubled party. That is apparently why, while Zhao's advisor Bao Tong was tried and sentenced for conspiracy, Zhao conspicuously escaped prosecution. This put Zhao in a similar position to that of Deng in the 1970s. In short, if Deng Xiaoping failed to push through his reform, Zhao might well reemerge through a coup.

For millions of Chinese in the cities and on the coast who were more directly affected by the shifts in government policy, the game was to wait and see. So long as reform and openness remained in the rhetoric of Beijing, there was hope. The private sector of China's industry and commerce persisted despite temporary hardship. The coastal provinces kept an increasing distance from the hard-line economic policy of Beijing. In cities such as Shengzhen, Guangzhou and Xiamen, economic reform moved cautiously forward.[39] In the countryside, nothing can turn the system back to the people's commune. In the cities, the managers of state-owned enterprises hesitated, their employees restless for the resumption of reform. Such a public mood presaged Beijing's renewed drive for openness starting in 1992.

COMING OUT OF CHAOS

The new leadership's lukewarm interest in continuous economic reform and lack of imagination angered Deng Xiaoping, and in Beijing he found himself in a situation not unlike Mao Zedong in the mid-1960s. He still had many supporters in the provinces, where the local economy had already been freed from central control and could not be put back into Chen Yun and Li Peng's cage. In March 1991, *Jiefang Ribao* (*Liberation Daily*) in Shanghai carried a series of articles by Huang Puping, who represented the municipal committee of the CCP. Calling for new ideas and new approaches in the reform of 1990s, the author insisted that keeping reform alive was the only way out for Shanghai's stagnant economy. He also invited foreign investment to the Shanghai area, at least indirectly challenging the conservative attitude of Beijing after June4, 1989 toward foreign investment in China. Moreover, he also advocated appointing true reformers in the government and removing double-dealers who put up hurdles to further economic reform.[40] *People's Daily* and *Beijing Daily* were unhappy but kept silent when they realized that Deng Xiaoping was behind these articles.[41]

Deng Xiaoping, who was apparently concerned with his place in history as well as the survival of the regime, broke out from semiretirement in early 1992 to visit South China, where he delivered talks containing a hidden threat to conservatives. Again the old man showed an incredible serenity of mind when talking about economic strategy and reaffirming the experience of the SEZs, especially Shenzhen. He asked the entire party to stay on the course laid down by the Third Plenum of the Eleventh Congress of the CCP because reform held the key to the party and regime's survival. Those who feared the comeback of capitalism because of the Dengist *glasnost*, he said contemptuously, misunderstood the basics Marxism. Showing no remorse for June 4, 1989, the old man nevertheless emphatically approved the progress between 1984 and 1988 when Zhao Ziyang was executing the economic reforms. The old guard of Chinese communism reiterated his economic pragmatism and political conservatism. He sent out a clear message that only success in economic progress could save the cause of socialism in China. Contrary to Lucian Pye's characterization,[42] Deng was unequivocal and he sounded ready for a showdown with anyone standing in his way.

At present, we are subject to the influence from the right as well as from the left. But it is the leftist ideas that are the most difficult to eradicate. There are still some theoreticians and politicians who bluff people with a big club. These people come from the left, not from the right. Leftism has some revolutionary coloration. [It is as if] the more leftist you are, the more revolutionary you will be. How destructive leftism was in the history of our party! In the wink of an eye a very good thing was undone. Rightism can destroy socialism; so can leftism. China of course has to guard against rightism. But leftism is the bigger threat. . . . It is leftist to see the economic sphere as the source of peaceful transformation.[43]

However, Deng met with virtually no opposition, for continuous economic reform was the desire of the majority of the Chinese people and many lower-level officials, at least in the coastal cities.[44] Meanwhile, the conservative reaction had more or less run out of steam.

The pent-up energy of the Chinese people since the Tiananmen erupted, this time with an unprecedented drive for money, since political reform remained a taboo. But Deng and his people were working at cross purposes. Deng wanted to salvage his party from total ruin by establishing credibility in the economy. As for millions of the Chinese people, material betterment becomes the only legitimate goal of life when democracy seems still remote and infeasible. Deng's logic was crystal clear: if he could lead the party to achieve economic success, his place in history would both be secure. After Tiananmen, he was most eager to leave China in prosperity. What happens after him would be other people's business.

Responding to popular sentiment and Beijing's need for limited relaxation, active thinking revived, at first in the party itself. *China's Leftist Peril: A Panoramic Historical Record* by Wen Yu (a pseudonym for several scholars of the CCP history) echoed Deng Xiaoping's talks warnings against leftism in the CCP. The realism and courage to liquidate the leftist peril in the history of the Communist party indicated the enormous dynamism of liberal thinking among the younger scholars in the CCP. The authors pointed out that ultra-leftism was the most important source of disaster for the Chinese people of today. As expected, the book made instant news in Beijing, warming the hearts of many, while enraging the conservatives in the capital. After a prompt reading of the book, Jiang Zemin ordered it banned for its "totally negative portrayal" of the party.[45]

Feeling more comfortable with both domestic and international situations, reformers even began to resume the image of enlightened despots. Such confidence was refracted an article in the January 11, 1993, issue of the *Director and Manager Daily* (*Changzhang jingli ribao*) by Hu Jiwei, a member of the Politburo of the CCP. Under the title, "Develop the Chinese Conception of Democracy to Facilitate Democratization in China" (*Chuangli zhongguo minzhu lilun, tuijin zhongguo minzhu jianshe*), Hu dwelt on the necessity of exploring ways to establish "a relatively correct and reasonable conception of Chinese democracy" through studies of reality as well as history, economy as well as politics, material things as well as spiritual matters, and foreign practices as well as Chinese methods. He advocated a society based on some consensus but at the same time allowing diverse values among its citizens. Surprisingly, this top official even said that the ruling party "must swear with remorse" that it would "never exercise ideological dictatorship." Hu's article at least partially reflected the awareness of public sentiments and the world political trends among the younger leaders of the ruling party. Like other authoritarian regimes in modern times, Chinese leaders are often compelled to recognize the need for a certain degree of democratization of the political system, although for them, democracy is rather a means to the end of socialism and modernization than a political goal in itself.[46]

China's intellectuals somehow recovered from their numbness and fear after Tiananmen. Seeing no hope for an immediate breakthrough in the political reforms, many plunged into the torrent of commercialization. There has obviously been a tacit understanding between the government and the educated elite that the latter would not openly challenge the legitimacy of the CCP while the party would leave them alone in their commercial adventures. Money can diffuse politics: this was the lesson that the Chinese government and people learned the hard way. To many intellectuals, who suffered from economic polarization since the early 1980s, this was a chance to pull themselves from years of destitution. The standard of living for most educators was below the national average. Appalling working conditions and a lack of benefits took their toll, especially among college professors, whose average life span is ten years shorter than the national average. At the same time, many were also expecting a greater voice in China's future. If a market economy is the inevitable goal, then money will translate into political power. The government was content, too, for it had at least gained a precious, if uneasy, truce to make necessary readjustment.

In any event, commercial economy and a market consciousness are laying the cornerstones in China for an overall openness and a modern civil society. While "xiahai" (the jump into the "ocean of commerce") has become a household term in mainland China, the tide predicts the emergence of a strong middle class and will once again produce new ideas to challenge the CCP's authoritarian rule.[47]

Out of the agony following the Tiananmen tragedy, China's reformers and the Chinese people developed a common ground, however fragile, on which to resume the temporarily halted economic reform. At the Fourteenth Congress of the CCP, a new party line crystallized. Hard political control combined with soft economic policy gained wide currency in the CCP apparatus and won the Chinese people's acquiescence. The Fourteenth Congress called for adherence to the party's basic line, as geared to new conditions, a tightening of party discipline, and an improvement in the party's leadership and administrative skills. Most noticeably, Jiang Zemin's report to the congress emphasized economic growth as the criterion for the party's policies. The reformers claimed a victory because the congress called for continuous reform while recognizing the need to fight corruption in the party and the government. The conservatives were undercut, for the reformers shared their political goals. It was a victory for Deng Xiaoping because, among other things, his thought was promoted as the new bible for Chinese communism, and his ideas about socialism with Chinese characteristics sounded the key note for the congress. The somewhat contradictory term, "socialist market economy" was enshrined in the party's constitution.[48] The result of the Fourteenth Congress suggested that not only did Deng Xiaoping find continuous reform to be the only way out of the impasse following Tiananmen, he also found enough supporters in the political establishment, including younger colleagues such as Tian Jiyun and Zhu Rongji, that even Jiang Zemin and Li Peng could not reverse the tide.

The conservatives were again muffled at the congress. Not only did they have to acquiesce to Deng Xiaoping's blueprint for China in the 1990s, they lost some of their most diedard comrades, such as Gao Di, He Jingzhi, and Wang Renzhi. The congress was also preceded by the disgrace of Yang Baibing whose rivals formed a strong bloc to topple him. After Tiananmen, Yang Baibing and his cohorts entered into the spotlight for China watchers as upstarts in the government and military. He seemed to be at the pinnacle of his political career during Deng Xiaoping's visit to south China in early 1992, when he loudly asked the military to wholeheartedly support the reform. However, to everybody's surprise, Yang Baibing was expelled from the Central Military Committee at the Fourteenth Congress. Jiang Zemin expectedly became chairman of the organ as chairman of the party, and Liu Huaqing and Chi Haotian were retained. The other members, such as Zhang Zhen, Zhang Wanlian, and Yu Yongbo were all new to this body. At the same time, Yang Shangkun reluctantly handed over the presidency of the state to Jiang Zemin. The expulsion of the Yang brothers apparently resulted from the growing feud between them and leaders of other powerful factions in China's military, especially the large military regions. It also indicated the rising power of professional officers in the PLA, who became increasingly important in the military as a result of the modernization program.[49]

The core of the new leadership, the Politburo, showed several prominent features. First, its members were young and professional, most having a college education (seven from the former Soviet Union and one from Czechoslovakia), and most majoring in technology and natural sciences. The composition of the leadership certainly reflected the will of Deng Xiaoping for sure, but even more it reflected China's political and economic conditions. All the Politburo members had experience in administrative affairs. Frictions among them aside, this was perhaps the best thing for which many Chinese could hope until Deng and Chen Yun quit the scene. At the same time, the political role of the military was reaffirmed in the fact that its members in the central committee increased from 16.5 percent to 23.2 percent of that body. By doing so, reformers further bound the PLA to the bandwagon of economic openness. With the loyalty of the military ensured, the leadership could carry out radical economic reforms while maintaining the necessary political stability.

The Fourteenth Congress and the interactions between the ruling party and Chinese society opened a new era of progress and uncertainty. Everywhere in China one can see Deng Xiaoping's admonition to his party, "If you don't adhere to the socialist road, if you don't follow the reforms, if you don't develop the economy, if you don't improve your livelihood, then the only way for you is death."[50] There is no doubt that the authority of the CCP is no longer based on an ideology but rather on its performance in administration, and especially its effort in pushing forward economic reforms. The relationship between the state and society in China is undergoing a profound transformation. The days when the state could control everything are gone and even the priority of the state is being challenged. The Communist regime must respond to the needs of society, especially those in the economic sphere. The growing power of societal and regional powers and the CCP's consequent dependence on economic progress indicate that China is moving toward a new authoritarianism.[51]

Indeed China today "is no longer a Communist country in any meaningful sense."[52] The Communist party is still in command, but its guiding ideology has decayed beyond repair. Even if it tried to revive its revolutionary philosophy, its effect would be minimal, for such philosophy and ethics had long ago lost any appeal to the people and would only help expose the gulf between the party's deeds and words. The government thus became what Peter M. Lee called a "statolatry state," or a government by functionaries. Lacking in moral superiority, such a government demonstrates a strong conservatism and a legalistic disposition. It can carry on a "passive revolution" in the sense that its policy will reflect more the exigencies of day-to-day business rather than a romantic approach to a glorious end. It is not an exaggeration to say that in the 1990's the business of the party is business.[53] China today had become a land of capitalist miracles, where yesterday's rice paddy becomes tomorrow's metropolis, and a thousand factories bloom.[54]

We are thus tempted to say that the shooting in Tiananmen saved the Chinese government from toppling and the Chinese Communist party from disintegrating as happened in the former Soviet Union and to the Russian Communist Party. However, the use of violence by no means restored the the ruling party's ideological authority and organizational cohesion. None of the top Chinese leaders still believe in communism in the pure sense of the term.[55] The sole objective of the party became survival through economic reform and continuous political repression. In such a political climate, Singapore, the tiny city-state of Southeast Asia became the Chinese leaders' Mecca, despite the obviously disparate situations of the two countries. Whether the post-Deng Xiaoping government can keep up the momentum of the economic reform is contingent on how well the new authoritarian government can achieve sustained economic growth without disintegrating from within.

NOTES

1. It was said that Wang resigned under pressure.

2. Other high-ranking officials who fell include Xu Shjie, party secretary of Hainan, and Yuan Geng, chairman of China's Merchants' Steamship Navigation Company of Shekou. Zhongguo xinwenshe, September 14, 1989, in *Summary of World Broadcasts/Far East/0563/B1/2*; ZGXWS, October 16, 1989, in *SWB/FE/0593/B2/7*; *South China Morning Post*, March 24, July 7, 1990; Chen Yige, "Zhonggong gaogan da diaodong de jincheng" (Great reshuffle at the top of the CCP), *Jiushi Niandai* (Nineteen-Nineties), September 1990, pp. 22–24; Qi Xin, "Renren dongtan bude de zhonggong gaocheng quanli yunzuo" (The restraining power operation at the top of the CCP), *Nineties*, May 1990, pp. 28–31.

3. Yi Ke, "Renmin Ribao de wange" (The Dirge of the *People's Daily*), *Zhongguo zhi Chun* (China Spring), October 1991, pp. 62–64.

4. Bi Hua, "Wenyijie daqingshuan kaishi le" (The great purge in the cultural sphere begins), *Nineties*, August 1989, pp. 100–102; Li Xiaozhuang, "Zuopiezi dangdao, dalu wentan xianru tongku qi" (China's literary circle suffers under the leftists), *Nineties*, May 1991, pp. 38–40.

5. It was said Jiang was strongly recommended by Deng Pufang, Deng Xiaoping's eldest son, for his political savvy.

6. China's police force increased to 1.4 million in 1990. Mao Shen, "Dalu wujing yuansheng zaidao" (Armed police in mainland China have many grievances), *Nineties*, June 1990, pp. 72–73.

7. Ibid.

8. Shi Hua, "Yishi minxin renzhang tianxia," (Still in power after losing the people's confidence), *Nineties*, November 1989, pp. 22–24; Lin Wei, "Zhonggong jili yingzao biaomian wending," (The CCP works hard to create the veneer of stability), *Nineties*, March 1990, pp. 32–34; Qi Xin, "Cong renda kan zhonggong de wending" (A glimpse into China's stability through the People's Congress), *Nineties*, April 1990, pp. 20–22; Xinhua News Agency, February 26, 1991, in *Summary of World Broadcasts/Far East/1032/C1/1*, March 28, 1991.

9. He Ping, "Jiafangjun de yexin he danxin" (Ambition and worry of the PLA), *China Spring*, April 1991, pp. 34–37.

10. Beijing Municipal Government, "Qingche zhenbao gongzuo fangan qingshi" (A proposed plan for rounding up and punishing rioters), quoted in He Ping, "Cong liusi da shoubu dao jiuyi da shenpan" (From the June 4, 1989, roundup to the great trial of 1991), *China Spring*, March 1991, pp. 17–23.

11. Liu Binyan, Ruan Ming and Xu Gang, *Tell the World: What Happened and Why*, trans. Henry L. Epstein (New York: Pantheon Books, 1989), pp. 128–129.

12. A system of community surveillance before 1949 in which villagers were required to watch each other and turn in criminals to the authorities.

13. Deng Xiaoping, "Women you xinxin ba zhongguo de shiqing zuode genghao" (We have the confidence to make things even better in China), *Deng Xiaoping Wenxuan* (*Selected works of Deng Xiaoping*) (Beijing: Renmin Press, 1993), 3:327.

14. The growth rate of foreign direct investment was only 5.7 percent in 1989 as compared to 42.8 percent in 1988 and 30.9 percent in 1987. See Z. S. Khan, "Patterns of Foreign Direct Investment in China," *World Bank Discussion Papers*, no. 130 (World Bank: Washington, D.C., September, 1991).

15. Deng Xiaoping, "Women you xinxin ba zhongguo de shiqing zuode genghao," *Selected Works*, 3:325–326; "Shehuizhuyi de zhongguo shui ye dongyao du liao" (No one can sway socialist China), in ibid, 328–329; "Jieshu yanjun de zhongmei guanxi yao you meiguo caiqu zhudong" (The United States should take the initiative to improve Sino-American relations), in ibid, 330–333.

16. The Television series "Yearning," broadcast in 1990, was a case in point.

17. Commentator, "Wodang de zhishi fenzi zhengce buhui gaibian" (The intellectual policy of our party will not change), *Renmin Ribao* (People's Daily), August 4, 1989.

18. Lin Wei, "Jushi jinzhang kunrao zhonggong" (Tension troubles the CCP), *Nineties*, September 1989, pp. 68–9.

19. Fu Deshai, "Chengmo zhongde xiwang," (Hopes in silence: Beijing University after June 4), *Ming Bao Monthly*, February 1990, pp. 41–42.

20. Deng Xiaoping, "Zhucheng yige shixing gaige de you xiwang de lingdao jiti" (Forming a pro-reform and promising leadership), *Selected Works*, 3:297–300; "Di sandai lingdao jiti de dangwu zhiji" (The urgent task for the third generation leadership), in ibid, 313–314; Yu Jianxing, "Yi jianshe you zhongguo teshe shehuizhuyi de lilun wei zhidao jiaqiang he gaijin dang de jianshe" (Strengthen and improve the organizational work of our party under the guidance of the conception of socialism with Chinese characteristics), *Qiushi*, July 1993, p. 7.

21. Xinshu Zhao & Peilu Shen, "Some Reasons Why the Party Propaganda Failed This Time," in Roger V. Forges, Luo Ning, and Wu Ten-bo, eds., *Chinese Democracy and the Crisis of 1989: Chinese and Aamerican Reflections* (Albany, N.Y.: State University of New York Press, 1993), pp. 323–326.

22. Lin Wei, "Zhonggong jili yunzao biaomian wending" (The CCP tries hard to create the veneer of stability), *Nineties*, March 1990, pp. 32–34.

23. Liu Binyan, *Tell the World*, p. 145.

24. Shi Hua, "Yishi minxin renzhang tianxia," (Still in power after losing the people's confidence), *Nineties*, November 1989, pp. 22–24. In Beijing, the audience gave a hilarious standing ovation duirng the performance of the *Red Lantern*, a model

Beijing opera sponsored by Madame. Mao duirng the Cultural Revolution, when the heroine sang, "I'll never quit the battle before all the wolves are killed."

25. Jin Wei, "Liusi zhounian fang Beijing" (Visit Beijing at the first anniversary of June 4), *Nineties*, July 1990, pp. 64–67; Yan Jiuding, "Zhongguo diyi dianshi zhubo—Du Xian" (Du Xian: China's no. 1 TV news anchor), *Minzhu Zhongguo* (Democratic China), May 1994, pp. 40–43.

26. Jude Howell, *China Opens Its Doors: The Politics of Economic Transition* (Hemel Hempstead: Harvester Wheatsheaf, 1993), p. 102.

27. Yi Ke, "Remin ribao de wange" (The dirge of the *People's Daily*), *China Spring*, October 1991, pp. 62–64.

28. Liu Binyan, "1991: zhongguo yin zhuan duoyun" (China's political situation in 1991: from overcast to cloudiness), *Ming Bao Monthly*, December 1991, p. 81.

29. Shi Hua, "Yishi minxin renzhang tianxia" (Still in power after losing the people's confidence), *Nineties*, November 1989, pp. 22–24.

30. China, State Statistics Bureau, "Dui dangqian jingji shenghuo zhong ruogan wenti de kanfa" (Comments on certain problems in the nation's economy), *People's Daily*, October 24, 1989; Lian Huawen, "Zhongguo jingji da huapo" (China's economy taking a nose dive), *Nineties*, November 1989, pp. 18–19; Lian Huawen, "Da Huapo xia de zhongguo jingji" (Chinese economy in recession), *Nineties*, January 1990, pp. 49–51. Zheng Zhuyun, "Liusi zhengjing beijing yu zhongguo dalu qiantu" (Sociopolitical Background of June 4th and the Future of Mainland China), Preface to *Tiananmen tusha beihou* (Behind the Tiananmen massacre), *Ming Bao Monthly*, June 1991, p. 13.

31. Lin Heng, "Zhonggong jili yunzao biaomian wending" (The CCP tries hard to create the veneer of stability), *Nineties*, March 1990, pp. 32–34.

32. See *People's Daily*, April 10, 1990, May 18, 1990; June 19, 1990; and July 10, 1990; also see Lin Nian, "Zhongguo dalu jingji haozhuan de beihou" (Behind the economic recovery of mainland China), *Ming Bao Monthly*, August 1990, pp. 12–14; Lian Huawen, "Zhongguo Jingji da huapo" (Chinese economy taking a nose dive), *Nineties*, November 1989, pp. 18–19.

33. Howell, *China Opens Its Doors*, pp. 93–94, 97.

34. Commentator, "Tian jiang jiang daren yu si zhidu ye" (The historical mission of socialism), *People's Daily*, August 23, 1991.

35. In 1991, both Jiang Zemin and Li Peng visited Moscow. See Howell, *China Opens Its Doors*, pp. 101–102.

36. *People's Daily*, July 1, 1991.

37. Deng Xiaoping, "Shicha Shanghai shi de tanhua" (Talks during a visit to Shanghai), *Selected Works*, 3:367; He Ping, "Guxi zhi qing he quanwei zhi zheng" (The seventieth birthday of the CCP and power struggle in Beijing), *China Spring*, August 1991, p. 10; also see China News Agency, "Deng Xiaoping's New Cat Thesis," July 3, 1991.

38. Liu Binyan, "1991, zhongguo yin zhuan duoyun" (China's political situation in 1991: from overcast to cloudiness), *Ming Bao Monthly*, December 1991, pp. 77–79; Howell, *China Opens Its Doors*, p. 100.

39. Howell, *China Opens Its Doors*, p. 96.

40. Huang Puping, "Gaige kaifang xuyao xin sixiang" (Reform and openness need new ideas), *Jiefang Ribao* (Liberation Daily), March 2, 1991; "Jiaqiang wumen de kaifang yishi" (Strengthen our sense of openness), *Jiefang Ribao* (Liberation Daily), March 22, 1991.

41. Deng Xiaoping, "Shicha Shanghai shi de tanhua" (Talks during a visit to shanghai), *Selected Works*, 3:366–367; He Ping, "Shanghai huangpuping he beijing keji re" (Shanghai's Huang Puping and Beijing's science and technology heat), *China Spring*, June 1991, pp. 10–13; Liu Binyan, "China's Political Situation in 1991: from Overcast to Cloudiness," *Ming Bao Monthly*, December 1991, pp. 77–82.

42. "Deng has been able to strengthen his authority from time to time by merely spreading rumors of his own cryptic quotations." Lucian W. Pye, *The Spirit of Chinese Politics* (Cambridge, Mass: Harvard University Press, 1992), p. 203.

43. Deng Xiaoping, "Zai wuchang, shengzhen, zhuhai, shanghai dengdi de tanhua yaodian" (Talks in Wuchang, Shenzhen, Zhuhai and Shanghai etc.: A Summary, Jan 18-Feb 21, 1992), *People's Daily* (Overseas edition), November 6, 1993.

44. *Nanfang Ribao* (South China Daily), March 28, 1992.

45. Wen Yu, *Zhongguo Zuohuo: Quanjing shi changpian lishi jishi* (China's leftist peril: A panoramic historical record) (Beijing: Zhaohua Press, 1993); Shu Si, "Zuofeng guanchuan zhonggong shi" (Leftism undergirds the history of the CCP), *Cheng Ming*, May 1993, pp. 40–43; Tian Zhen, "*Zhongguo Zuohuo* yingqi de qianglie fanxiang" (Strong reactions to *China's Leftist Peril*), *Cheng Ming*, May 1993, pp. 37–39.

46. Hu Jiwei, "*Chuangli zhongguo minzhu lilun tuijin zhongguo minzhu jianshe*" (Develop the Chinese conception of democracy to facilitate democratization in China), *Changzhang Jingli Ribao* (Director and Manager Daily), January 11, 1993; see also Samuel P. Huntington, *The Third Wave: Democratization in the late Twentieth century* (Norman and London: University of Oklahoma Press, 1991), pp. 56–57.

47. Ming Lei, "Jing qiaoqiao de geming—siyuan jinghua shifanglu" (A quiet revolution: A visit to Beijing in April), *Ming Bao Monthly*, May 1993, pp. 22–24; Liu Minghua, *Shiji Xuanfeng: Rencai da taowang* (Hurrican of the century: The great flight of talents) (Chongqing, China: Chongqing University Press, 1993), pp. 38–52; Huntington, *Third Wave*, p. 66.

48. Jiang Zemin, "Report at the Fourteenth Congress of the CCP," *Qiushi* 12 (1992): 5; Yu Jianxing, "yi jianshe you zhongguo teshe shehuizhuyi wei zhidao jiaqiang he gaijin dang de jianshe" (Strengthen and improve the organizational work of our party under the guidance of the conception of socialism with Chinese characteristics), *Qiushi* 7 (1993): 5–12; Zhang Xihong, "Hou deng xiaoping shidai yu xinjiapo moshi" (The post-Deng Xiaoping era and the Singapore mode), *Ming Bao Monthly*, November 1992,

pp. 13–14; Wu Kangmin, "shisi da yu deng xaioping shidai (The Fourteenth Congress and the Deng era), *Ming Bao Monthly*, November 1992, pp. 20–22.

49. He Pin, "Shisida renshi anpai toushi" (Personnel reshuffling at the Fourteenth Congress of the CCP), *China Spring*, December 1992, pp. 14–17; Yang Manke, "Jiefangjun zouxiang ganzheng" (Will the PLA intervene in Chinese politics?), ibid, pp. 18–19; "Zongzhengzhibu de renshi xin buju" (Recent personnel changes in the general political department of the PLA), *Beijing Spring*, August 1993, pp. 39–41.

50. Deng, "Talks in Wuchang, Shenzhen, Zhuhai, Shanghai," *People's Daily*, November 6, 1993.

51. Deng Yong, "Zhongguo zheng kuaxiang xin quanwei zhuyi" (China is moving toward new authoritarianism), *Beijing Spring*, August 1993, p. 38. Others disagree, believing that the Chinese government is post-totalitarian and that a new authoritarianism cannot rise under a communist totalitarian regime. In addition, there is the possibility of the rise of democracy in a free economy brought about by reforms under a totalitarian regime. Therefore, people have to accept the combination of political totalitarianism and economic reform. See, Hua Ziyi, "Zhongguo bu keneng kuaxiang xin quanwei zhuyi" (New authoritarianism cannot rise in China), *Beijing Spring*, June 1993, pp. 23–26; Yuan Zhiming, "Wei Xin quanweizhuyi bianhu" (An apology for new authoritarianism), *Cheng Ming*, November 1991, p. 15; see also Yuan Zhiming, "Zaiwei xin quanweizhuyi bianhu" (Second apology for new authoritarianism), *Cheng Ming*, March 1993, p. 17.

52. Nicholas D. Kristof, "China Riddle: Life Improves though Repression Persists," *New York Times*, September 7, 1993.

53. Peter Nan-shong Lee, "Deng Xiaoping and the 1989 Tiananmen Square Incident," in Peter Li, Steven Mark, and Marjorie H. Li eds., *Culture and Politics in China: An Anatomy of Tiananmen Square* (New Brunswick, N.J.: Transaction Publishers, 1991), p. 174; Kristof, "China Sees Market-Leninism as Way to Future," *New York Times*, September 6, 1993; also see Nicholas D. Kristof, "China Riddle," *New York Times*.

54. Paul Theroux, "Going to See the Dragon," *Harper's*, October 1993, pp. 33–56.

55. Kristof, "China Sees Market-Leninism as Way to the Future," *New York Times*, September 6, 1993.

6

Conclusion: The Transition and Beyond

Throughout this book, the following basic assumption has been made: changes in public attitudes toward and perception of a polity resulting from changing sociopolitical preconditions (such as the consequences of polity's ruling) can cause a change in the nature of the polity. From these assumptions, our major hypotheses have been developed: (1) if the overall sociopolitical conditions in China, as independent variables, change significantly over a period of time, the public attitudes toward the Communist regime will also change; and (2) as public attitudes change fundamentally, the nature of the regime, as a dependent variable, will eventually change. These two hypotheses postulate two causal relationships among the variables or sociopolitical factors: one is between the overall sociopolitical conditions, including the social-economic consequences of party policies, and public attitudes, in which the former constitute the independent variable and the latter, the dependent variable; and the other is between public attitudes and the nature of the regime, where the former becomes the independent variable and the latter, the dependent variable.

The early chapters of this book have explored these hypotheses, examining China's sociopolitical change since the end of the Cultural Revolution as a transition from a totalitarian to an authoritarian regime. This transition has been identified through the discussion on the changes in the three key variables—sociopolitical conditions, the masses' attitudes, and the nature of the regime after the Cultural Revolution and during Deng's reforms. Specifically, the significant change in the nature of the Communist regime since the Cultural Revolution has been examined by looking at changes in the two key indicators—the status of the Party leadership and that of the official ideology, with which the regime officially identifies itself. The findings of the early chapters indicated that because of profound changes in China's sociopolitical conditions, and hence in public attitudes after the Cultural

Revolution and during the post–Mao reform, China's current Communist regime underwent a transition from Maoist totalitarian rule to Dengist authoritarian rule. In this concluding chapter, it seems necessary to highlight some important findings of the previous chapters and then to delineate possible directions of the current regime in line with the theoretical assumptions applied earlier in this book.

THE TRANSITION REVISITED

All changes in public attitudes and the nature of the regime were initiated by shifts in sociopolitical conditions. These conditions in China had changed dramatically by the end of the Cultural Revolution: hundreds of thousands of people from all social strata were persecuted mentally or physically; the national economy was on the brink of bankruptcy; and people's living standard failed to improve or even declined in many areas. Radical policies during the Cultural Revolution failed to bring about the utopia the totalitarian regime had promised at the beginning of this "mass movement." Rather, the consequences of these policies estranged a great number of the Chinese people from the Communist Party and caused serious doubts about the official ideology. In short, the Cultural Revolution did irreparable damage to the Party's image and its absurdity manifested the fallacy of Mao Zedong Thought. As a result, most people began to change their attitudes toward the party and the official ideology. This attitudinal change was reflected in some early political incidents, such as the April 5th Protest of 1976 and the Democracy Wall Movement of 1978–1979.

The post–Mao political and economic reforms initiated in 1979 thus can be seen as the regime's response to popular discontent after the Cultural Revolution. These reforms, as a catalyst, further affected people's thinking and drastically accelerated the transition from a totalitarian to an authoritarian regime. This change was signified by the fact that both the party leadership organizations and the official ideology deteriorated; consequently, the regime was compelled to resort to force to suppress the mass movement of 1989.

It is worth noting that the change in the nature of the regime, which seemingly occurred as the result of the political and economic reforms, actually contradicted Deng's original political purposes: to tranquilize the society and create a consensus among the people, hence reinforcing the one-party rule of the CCP. The reasons for such a contradiction between the ends and means of the reforms can be found in two aspects: one related to the fundamental agent of the reforms, and the other to the tactics of the reforms as applied by the leadership.

The fundamental agent of the reforms is the public's demand for better living conditions and greater political freedom. As Su Shaozhi, a leading

Chinese dissident, pointed out in early 1989, "No Chinese of conscience can fail to recognize the fact that democracy and science in China today are extremely incomplete. On the difficult road to democracy and science in China, feudal despotism has always been the number one enemy."[1] He believed, therefore, that "the open door and reform in China should be conducted under the banner of democracy and science and should not be stamped with any other narrowly defined nationalist or ideological colors. Otherwise, there will be no true modernization."[2] Although the conceptualization of democracy in China as a political system or philosophy has never been as complete as in the West, after the Cultural Revolution and during the reform, increasing numbers of the Chinese people, especially the urban youth, began to develop a somewhat liberal mentality. This kind of mentality, of course, was not equivalent to a clear understanding of the political and social meanings of Democracy, because the deeply rooted Chinese political culture, which generally has a strong preference for totalitarianism, never provided a permissible sociopolitical environment for genuine democratic socialization. While the mentality was vague in defining the concept, it overwhelmingly pointed to one general direction—the attainment of a more humane society with material betterment and political liberalization. This general tendency was dramatized in the post–Mao era by such events as the Democracy Wall Movement of 1978–1979, the Student Demonstrations of 1986–1987, and the Democracy Movement of 1989, in which a multiparty system, direct popular election of national leaders, and freedom of petition were widely demanded.[3]

Such public sentiment following the Cultural Revolution, as hypothesized in Chapter 1, constituted the agent for fundamental changes in the regime and also for the irresistible social forces for reform. Deng Xiaoping, who himself was a victim of ultra-leftism under Mao during the Cultural Revolution, proved to be quite sensitive to this public mentality. He repeatedly told the party both before and during the reform that it was imperative for the party-state to meet public demands by improving people's standards of living. For instance, during his southern inspection tour in early 1992, Deng told a group of high-ranking provincial leaders that "if we don't carry out reform and an open-door policy, develop the economy, and improve people's living standard, there is only a dead end."[4] After the ten-year upheaval of the Cultural Revolution, Deng and his associates had reached a consensus that their ruling positions inevitably relied on public feeling and support. There were two major reasons for them to have this consensus. First, because of their personal suffering during the Cultural Revolution, they disliked the ultra-left policies implemented by Mao during that period. Thus, they could easily find a common ground between their political intentions and the public mentality that was antithetical to the ultra-left policies.

Second, these leaders were acutely aware that their personal popularity was no match for that of Mao, as they had always been perceived by the public as a group of secondary leaders within the Communist regime until the time of Mao's death. Thus, due to their lack of self-confidence, Deng and his associates were forced to be more responsive to the public sentiment. Their lack of confidence is well demonstrated by the fact that when Deng and his associates forsook most of Mao's policies, they never denounced Mao as Nikita Khrushchev denounced Stalin. Instead, they keep exalting Mao as a great leader and preserving, at least nominally, part of the body of ideas known as Mao Zedong Thought.[5] The combination of these two reasons led, in the post–Cultural Revolution era, to a leadership that was more sensitive to the changes in public sentiment, and more responsive to people's needs. In short, looking back to the process of the reform, we can safely say that the fundamental agent of the reform was the public mentality, to which the leadership had to respond when it tried to strengthen its position and revitalize the cause of socialism and communism following the traumatic Cultural Revolution.

While the intention of Deng and his supporters for the reform and the public mentality did converge, they also differed in some significant ways. Whereas many people spurned the ultra-left policies of the Cultural Revolution as did the new leadership, they expected at the beginning of the reform that the officialdom would institutionalize political freedoms by establishing regular dialogue between the government and the public, rigid scrutiny of officials, popular elections of leaders at least at the local level, and fair competition in economic activities. These expectations actually were articulated in the Democracy Wall Movement of 1978–1979, the Student Demonstrations of 1986–1987, and later in the Democracy Movement of 1989. However, Deng and his associates believed that the foremost goal of the reform was to establish or reestablish the "socialism with Chinese Characteristics" under the one-party rule of the CCP, rather than to form a democratic society. For them, political liberalization in some degree was only a tactic to gain public support at a time. This kind of political liberalization, therefore, could be abandoned as a tactic according to political expediency. In fact, during the reform, the leadership halted the liberalization frequently by launching several nationwide political campaigns, such as the Anti-Spiritual Pollution Campaign of 1983–1984 and the Anti-Bourgeois Liberalization Campaign of 1985.[6] The distance or contradiction between public expectations about the reform and the leaders' intentions proved to be one of the major sources of China's sociopolitical instability. The Democracy Movement of 1989, which arose in some major Chinese cities, best manifested these conflicts between the different ideas on reform from of the rulers and the ruled.

The potential political instability, rooted in the difference between the leaders' and public's understandings of the reform, was also aggravated by a series of policies implemented by Deng and his associates during the reform. These policies were initiated mainly based on Deng's pragmatic intent to gain short-term popular support for his leadership: As long as the CCP could improve economic conditions, the Chinese people's acceptance of party control could be assured.[7] The near-sighted expediency behind these policies eventually caused highly unpredictable political consequences for the leadership itself, which contradicted the original intent of the reform. As discussed in Chapters 3 and 4, while the political reform was designed to remove the ideological and political impediments for the pursuit of rational economic policies and recreate among the people a new consensus favorable to the regime, its serious side-effects were the erosion of the previous monolithic party leadership, especially the party's grass-roots apparatus, and of the official ideology. While the economic reform was intended as the major vehicle to boost the new leadership's popularity among the people, its by-products, such as economic polarization between the new rich and poor, high inflation, and official profiteering, brought about grievances among the people. As illustrated in Chapter 4, the sociopolitical uncertainty in late 1989 due to those side-effects following the ten-year reform finally shook the very foundations on which the regime had relied. The reform consequently ran counter to the original intention of the leadership: it destroyed the two mighty ruling pillars from under the post–Mao regime—the monolithic party leadership and the strong official ideology—making the regime weaker in the face of popular movements. As a result, the totalitarian regime was finally transformed into an authoritarian one, which depended on the use of force for its survival, as was well demonstrated in the Tiananmen Incident of 1989.

Looking back to the entire process of this political transition, we may generalize that the fundamental agent of any significant political change is public attitude, which varies in response to the consequences of a regime's rule as an important part of the ever-changing sociopolitical conditions. In the face of shifting public attitudes, the leadership of a regime will be eventually compelled by public attitudes to take the initiative in liberalizing politics and the economy. Such sociopolitical reforms, which are intended to maintain the party's legitimacy, in turn become a catalyst for further political transformation. As Samuel Huntington pointed out after observing many cases of such reforms in the developing countries, the reforms initiated by rulers had often not been the "outcome leaders desire most but may be the outcome that is least unacceptable."[8] In the case of political changes in China since the Cultural Revolution, the outcome of political and economic liberalization in the late 1970s and the entire 1980s was a political transition from a totalitarian regime to an authoritarian regime. This outcome is a far cry from what Deng and his supporters intended, because an authoritarian regime is more difficult to maintain and less stable than a totalitarian regime due to the lack of pervasive and effective ruling tools—strong party leadership and official ideology. However, it is the "least unacceptable" outcome, based on the fact that, at least Deng and his associates still remain in power.

PROSPECTS FOR THE NEW AUTHORITARIAN REGIME

The early chapters of this book define China's new regime after the Tiananmen Massacre of 1989 as an authoritarian regime, according to its prevalent institutional and structural attributes. This regime was characterized by weak party leadership and loose organizations, which were ineffective at controlling and monitoring the people's actions, and a loosely defined official ideology, which was too weak to provide any long-term moral values for society and therefore inadequate to support any absolute rule of the regime. Because of these attributes, the Chinese government since Tiananmen has relied almost solely on coercion and "economic miracles" for its existence.

For the current leadership, while the coercion stands ready as a "club" at all times to punish any dissenting behavior that might publicly threaten the legitimacy of the regime, the economic miracles, as a "carrot," are intended to placate the people. While coercion is necessary, if insufficient, to maintain "social stability," economic success is imperative in order to gain popularity among the people. The Chinese leaders have also repeatedly told the public that "economic growth and social stability are mutually promoted and integrated."[9] In fact, however, the "economic growth" and "social stability" do not necessarily interact positively, as the 1989 Tiananmen Incident proved.

Economic growth and social stability have time and again been underscored by the current leadership as the foremost sociopolitical conditions for "socialism with Chinese characteristics."[10] While this term has never been clearly or systematically defined by the leadership, it has been used as a catch-all concept to justify all kinds of official policies and initiatives in recent years. It is valuable to tackle the true meanings of this concept to help understand the sociopolitical goals of the current regime.

Upon reviewing official documents and speeches directly or indirectly fleshing out this vague concept, one can find that the policy and institutional implications of the "socialism with Chinese characteristics" are two-fold. On the one hand, "socialism" denotes the one-party rule of the CCP and predominant state-ownership of the means of production. The "Chinese characteristics," on the other hand, encompass all kinds of *pragmatic* policy initiatives, which are deemed "applicable" by Deng and his associates to the Chinese reality but do not conflict with the one-party rule or a predominant state-ownership of the means of production. According to Deng Xiaoping, the essential task of socialism is to "develop productive forces," and "continuously improve people's material life," because the current China's "backward economy" in China has hindered the improvement of the people's living standards and hence threatened the Communist one-party rule.[11] To develop a national economy, Deng believes, any economic policies should be considered legitimate and viable, so long as they do not directly contradict the two major principles of "socialism" (namely, the one-party rule and state-ownership of the means of production). Policies such as "implementation of the market mechanism," "a limited stock market," and "indirect government intervention in the economy" can be capitalist in nature. When Deng inspected several coastal cities in South China in early 1992, he cited Shenzhen as one of the best examples to illustrate "socialism with Chinese characteristics." He believes that the Shenzhen Special Economic Zone is still "socialist," because "state-owned enterprises play the main role, foreign investments constitute only one-fourth [of the local economy]," and these foreign investments are still "restricted by our national political and economic systems."[12]

Along the same line, the Third Plenum of the Fourteenth Congress of the CCP, held in November 1993, called for the nationwide establishment of the "socialist market economic system," allowing the entire national economy to operate with the market mechanism. The plenum instructed that governments at all levels should transform their functions from direct or micro control to indirect or macro adjustment of the economy through "economic and legal measures." It reiterated, however, that the leadership of the CCP should be "strengthened and improved" through a revitalization of party organizations at the basic level.[13] Whether the party leadership can be "strengthened and improved" to its strength in Mao's era is debatable, but it seems clear that the current leadership is still determined to monopolize the ultimate political authority.

In short, as the current leadership has defined, the "socialism with Chinese characteristics" denotes one-party rule with tight political control, on the one hand, and high-speed economic growth with even greater economic freedom, on the other. At first glance, this formula seems an optimal and well-balanced means by which the regime can maintain its legitimacy at least in the short run: society can be stabilized by the tight political control, and the CCP's ruling position can be strengthened by the high rate of economic growth and economic freedom. Thinking about it carefully, however, we could detect some latent crises behind this political formula.

First, there still is a question as to whether and how the regime can maintain social stability through tight political control in the long run, since it has already lost its two mighty tools—effective party organizations and strong official ideology—and has only coercion left at its disposal. The biggest disadvantage of relying on coercion to govern is that the regime cannot efficiently prevent potential political upheavals in advance since coercion has little power to channel people's thinking. That would potentially allow popular discontent and even political agitation to grow out of hand. The Mass Democracy Movement of 1989 was a classic case in which the regime could neither prevent people from staging such mass demonstrations nor persuade them to evacuate the streets, due to a lack of functional party organizations and powerful ideology. The massacre by the government following the mass demonstrations actually led to a mounting hatred for and distrust in the leaders.

Such antipathy among the public, in turn, became fuel for future social upheavals. For instance, while "swift arrests and heavy sentences" were conducted by the government to round up any remaining dissenters, many people vowed in secret that they would seize any opportunity for their revenge on the government for its atrocities. Sociopolitical stability under the new authoritarian regime, therefore, still remains unachieved, as "tight political control" through coercion alone does not seem to be a cure-all.

Second, high-speed economic growth does not necessarily justify and reinforce the one-party rule. Based on their observations, Joan Nelson and Samuel Huntington argued that authoritarian regimes in developing countries could follow a so-called "vicious circle"—starting with "suppression of political participation, rapid economic growth, and increased socioeconomic inequality, leading to mounting popular discontent and a participation 'explosion' against the regime."[14] Their argument was once again proved by events in China during the 1979–1989 period. Deng and his supporters started their reform with a suppression of participation by political dissenters and with high-speed economic growth. They ended up in 1989 with serious socioeconomic polarization between the new rich and poor, which led to popular discontent and mass demonstrations against their rule. Now, the current Chinese government calls for tighter political control and more rapid economic growth, while allowing very few people to become rich or richer. According to Deng, this "basic Party line will be held for a hundred years and cannot be changed."[15] According to his twisted logic, Deng even believed that the current regime could survive the upheaval of June 4, 1989, just through the "achievement" of this basic party line.[16] If the current party line still remains the same as, or similar to, that during the early reforms, however, it seems very likely that the regime will repeat the "vicious circle" in which one-party rule will be once again faced with popular discontent and mass movements resulting from the combination of political suppression and growing economic inequality. Then, the regime will again have to resort to coercion. In any case, high-speed economic growth alone cannot provide legitimacy for the regime, nor can it save the regime from sociopolitical instability.

In short, "socialism with Chinese characteristics," while having very little reference to Marxist orthodoxy, is simply a Chinese version of authoritarianism. The current regime, however, will not be immune to the problems inherent in authoritarianism, such as cyclical political upheaval, excessive reliance on coercion, and socioeconomic inequality, unless the leadership substantially changes policies such as "tight political control."

The foreseeable future for this regime under the banner of "socialism with Chinese characteristics" depends on at least three sociopolitical factors. The first is whether the regime can institutionalize formal and legal channels for political participation, especially by moderate opposition forces. If the regime allows at least moderate opposition forces to participate in the policy-making process through institutionalized channels, it may avoid or at least revise timely unpopular policies, thereby preventing an explosion of popular grievances. This choice to further liberalize the political system will depend on the adaptability of the ruling party in the face of a future public demand for greater freedom. After more than four decades of one-party rule, the Guomindang on Taiwan had already adapted itself to the changing sociopolitical environment by sharing power with other moderate oppositions in a quasi-legislative branch. Needless to say, ruling Communist parties in Eastern Europe had done the similar things. It is, therefore, not entirely inconceivable that the CCP could adapt itself to China's future political environment by sharing power with other moderate political groups especially after Deng's death, since the current CCP leadership embraces a substantial number of technocrats, such as Zhu Rongji, Tian Jiyun, Qiao Shi, and Li Ruihuan, who are ideologically more flexible and do not have as much stake in the old political establishment as Deng's generation. In the foreseeable future, however, the CCP will no doubt try its best to retain supremacy in the government while carefully determining the degree of tolerance of an opposition.

The second factor is whether the current regime could distribute social wealth in a more equitable manner as it continues with high-speed economic development. If the regime gradually establishes a direct and progressive taxation system and a comprehensive programs for social security and welfare, the socioeconomic inequality stemming from the ongoing reforms could be substantially reduced. With a more equitable system for the distribution of wealth, the regime could not only appease the citizenry but also lay down a healthy socioeconomic basis for further economic growth. In fact, there are positive signs that the current regime has recently realized the importance of socioeconomic equality and attempted to do something about it. At the Third Plenum of the Fourteenth Congress of the CCP, the party leaders decided to continue to "avoid polarization due to extremely high incomes of a few people by implementing appropriate taxation system."[17] Most recently, the government announced the newly revised Personal Income Tax Law, which came into effect on January 1, 1994. This law further breaks the personal income taxes into nine tax brackets, with 5 percent as the lowest tax rate and 45 percent as the highest.[18] While the implementation of the new Personal Income Tax Law still remains yet to be seen, the effort to establish a better tax system indicates that the Chinese leaders, especially the technocrats, learned a lesson from the Tiananmen incident of 1989, which was triggered largely by socioeconomic inequality. Thus, it is not unlikely that the current regime could make even more serious efforts to achieve socioeconomic equality.

The last factor is whether the current party leadership will continue to predominate over the military as a whole (*dang zhihui qiang*), especially after Deng's death. If the military is firmly under the central control of the party, it cannot independently address its own interests (should they differ from those of the party) by interfering in political debates within the party ruling circle. Without military intervention, then, the party leadership, which is now composed of younger and more liberal individuals than in previous years, could have more freedom to pursue and implement politically and economically flexible policies, such as letting moderate oppositions participate in politics and distributing social wealth more equally. While the party leaders could still use the military to suppress popular movements, as they did with the mass democracy movement of 1989, the military would not act on its own to seriously disturb policy-making within the party. In fact, at the Eighth Conference of the National People's Congress, held in March 1993, the party chief Jiang Zemin was "elected" both as the President of the state and the Chairman of the Central Military Committee.[19] On the other hand, the former military heads Yang Shangkung and his brother in-law, Yang Baibing, who seemed to have a strong tendency to interfere in politics, lost power to Liu Huaqing and Zhang Zhen, who were deemed to be more moderate, professional, and less politically ambitious, and who now conduct the daily business of the military.[20] Such recent political developments indicate that the military is still under the firm control of the party leadership, and in the near future is unlikely to split with the party and to create social instability, such as a civil war.

Thus far, the current development in these policy areas seems to be driving the current one-party authoritarian regime toward a more technocrat-oriented polity. While this polity could share the major characteristics of authoritarianism, such as ineffective party organization and weak (or non-existent) official ideology, it likely could provide more opportunities for political participation by moderate opposition forces as well as implement more flexible policies. Thus, we could reasonably delineate the path of China's political change since the Cultural Revolution with this tentative chronological formula: After a transition from totalitarianism to authoritarianism, the current Chinese polity is moving toward what Lucian Pye calls a "dominant-party democracy,"[21] which could involve competition for power but not alternation in power, as well as participation in elections, although participation in office is only allowed for those in the "dominant" party.

NOTES

1. Su Shaozhi et al., "What Will the Year 1989 Tell Us?" in Suzanne Ogden, Kathleen Hartford, Lawrence Sullivan, and David Zweig, eds., *China's Search for Democracy: The Student and Mass Movement of 1989* (Armonk, NY: M. E. Sharpe, 1992), p. 27. The original Chinese version of this article was published in *Zhongguo Qingnian* (China Youth), January 1989, pp. 2–3.

2. Ibid., p. 29.

3. See James C. F. Wang, *Contemporary Chinese Politics: An Introduction*, 4th ed. (Englewood Cliffs, N.J.: Prentice Hall, 1992), pp. 225–232.

4. Deng Xiaoping, *Deng Xiaoping Wenxuan* (Selected Works of Deng Xiaoping), (Beijing, China: People's Press, 1993) 3: 370.

5. See "On Questions of Party History-Resolution on Certain Questions in the History of Our Party Since the Founding of the People's Republic of China," (adopted by the Sixth Plenum of the Eleventh Central Committee of the Chinese Communist Party on June 27, 1981), *Beijing Review*, July 6, 1981.

6. See Wang, *Contemporary Chinese Politics*, pp. 216–221.

7. See Hsi-Sheng Ch'i, *Politics of Disillusionment: The Chinese Communist Party under Deng Xiaoping, 1978–1989* (Armonk, N.Y.: M. E. Sharpe, 1991), p. 257.

8. Samuel P. Huntington, *The Third Wave: Democratization in the Late Twentieth Century* (Norman: University of Oklahoma Press, 1991), p. 108.

9. "CCP Central Committee's Decisions on the Questions of the Establishment of Socialist Market Economic System" (adopted at the Third Plenum of the Fourteenth Congress of the CCP), *Guangmin Ribao*, November 17, 1993.

10. For Deng's early definition of the socialism with Chinese Characteristics, see Deng, *Selected Works*, 3:62–66.

11. Ibid., p. 63.

12. Ibid., pp. 372–373

13. "CCP Central Committee's Decisions on the Questions of the Establishment of Socialist Market Economic System" (adopted at the Third Plenum of the Fourteenth Congress of the CCP), *Guangmin Daily*, November 17, 1993.

14. Samuel P. Huntington, "The Goals of Development," in Myron Weiner and Samuel Huntington, eds., *Understanding Political Development* (Boston: Little, Brown and Company, 1987), p. 21.

15. Deng, *Selected Works*, 3: 370–371.

16. See ibid., p. 371.

17. See "CCP Central Committee's Decisions on the Questions of the Establishment of Socialist Market Economic System" (adopted at the Third Plenum of the Fourteenth Congress of the CCP), *Guangmin Daily*, November 17, 1993.

18. See "After the Implementation of the 'Personal Income Tax Law'," *Renmin Ribao* (People's Daily), December 25, 1993.

19. See *People's Daily*, March 29, 1993.

20. See Da Qiran, "Would the Military Interfere in Politics?" *Jiushi Niantai* (Nineties), September 1993, p. 36.

21. See Lucian W. Pye with Mary W. Pye, *Asian Power and Politics: The Cultural Dimensions of Authority* (Cambridge, Mass.: Harvard University Press, 1985); Lucian Pye, "Asia 1986—An Exceptional Year," *Freedom at Issue*, January-February 1987; and Huntington, *The Third Wave*, pp. 300–307.

Selected Bibliography

NEWSPAPERS AND PERIODICALS

Bashi Niandai (Eighties)
Beijing Review
Beijing Zhichun (Beijing Spring)
Cheng Ming
China Daily
China Journal
Guangming Ribao (Guangmin Daily)
Jiefang Ribao (Liberation Daily)
Jiushi Niandai (Nineties)
Liaowang
Ming Bao Monthly
Qishi Niandai (Seventies)
Qiushi
Renmin Ribao (People's Daily)
Shijie Jingji Daobao (World Economy Herald)
Zhongguo Zhichun (China Spring)

BOOKS AND ARTICLES

Almond, Gabriel A. "The Civic Culture Concept," in Roy C. Macridis and Bernard E. Brown, eds., *Comparative Politics: Notes and Readings*. Pacific Grove, Calif.: Brooks/Cole Publishing Company, 1990.

Bachman, David, and Dali L. Yang, eds. and trans. *Yan Jiaqi and China's Struggle for Democracy*. Armonk, N.Y.: M. E. Sharpe, 1991.

Barnett, A. Doak, and Ralph N. Clough, eds. *Modernizing China: Post–Mao Reform and Development.* Boulder, Colo.: Westview Press, 1986.

Bernstein, Thomas P. *Up to the Mountains and Down to the Villages.* New Haven, Conn.: Yale University Press, 1977.

Bo, Yibo. *Ruogan Zhongda Juece yu Shijian de Huigu* (Reflections on Some Important Decisions and Events) 2 vols. Beijing: Zhongyang Dangxiao Press, 1993.

Bodde, Derk. *Chinese Thought, Society, and Science.* Honolulu: University of Hawaii Press, 1991.

Brugger, Bill, ed. *China: The Impact of the Cultural Revolution.* New York: Barnes and Noble Books, 1978.

Brugger, Bill, and David Kelly. *Chinese Marxism in the Post–Mao Era.* Stanford, Calif.: Stanford University Press, 1990.

Burns, John. "Local Cadre Accommodation to the 'Responsibility System' in Rural China." *Pacific Affairs*, 58, no. 4 (Winter 1985–1986): 614–617.

Burns, John P., and Stanley Rosen, eds. *Policy Conflicts in Post–Mao China: A Documentary Survey with Analysis.* Armonk, N.Y.: M. E. Sharpe, 1986.

Burton, Charles. *Political and Social Change in China since 1978.* Westport, Conn.: Greenwood Press, 1990.

Central Committee of the Chinese Communist Party. "CCP Central Committee's Decisions on the Questions of the Establishment of Socialist Market Economic System" (adopted at the Third Plenum of the Fourteenth Congress of the CCP). *Guangmin Ribao*, November 17, 1993.

_____ ."On Questions of Party History-Resolution on Certain Questions in the History of Our Party since the Founding of the People's Republic of China" (adopted by the Sixth Plenum of the Eleventh Central Committee of the Chinese Communist Party on June 27, 1981). *Beijing Review*, 27 (July 6, 1981).

_____ . "Communiqué of the Third Plenum of the Eleventh Central Committee of the Communist Party of China." *Beijing Review* (December 29, 1978).

_____ . *Shiyijie sanzhong quanhui yilai zhongyao wenxian Xuandu* (Selected Readings of Major Documents since the Third Plenum of the Eleventh Central Committee). Beijing, China: People's Press, 1979.

Chan, Anita. *Children of Mao: Personality Development and Political Activism in the Red Guard Generation.* Seattle: University of Washington Press, 1985.

Chang, Parris. *Radicals and Radical Ideology in China's Cultural Revolution.* New York: Columbia University Press, 1973.

Chang, Y. C. *Factional and Coalition Politics in China: The Cultural Revolution and Its Aftermath.* New York: Praeger, 1976.

Chao, Zenyao. *Yongdong De Dachao: Zhongguo Shichang Jingji Daguan* (Gigantic Wave: A Grant Sight of China's Market Economy). Xian, China: Northwest University Press, 1993.

Che, Muqi. *Beijing Turmoil: More than Meets the Eye.* Beijing, China: Foreign Languages Press, 1990.

Cheng, Chu-yuan. *Behind the Tiananmen Massacre: Social, Political, and Economic Ferment in China.* Boulder, Colo.: Westview Press, 1990.

Ch'i, Hsi-sheng. *The Politics of Disillusionment: The Chinese Communist Party under Deng Xiaoping, 1978–1989.* Armonk, N.Y.: M. E. Sharpe, 1991.

Da, Qiran. "Would the Military Interfere in Politics?" *Jiushi Niandai (The Nineties),* (September 1993): 36–37.

Deng, Rong. *Wode fuqin Deng Xiaoping* (My Father Deng Xiaoping). Vol. 1. Beijing, China: Zhongyang Wenxian Press, 1993.

Deng, Xiaoping. *Deng Xiaoping Wenxuan* (Selected Works of Deng Xiaoping). Vol. 3. Beijing, China: People's Press, 1993

_____. *Deng Xiaoping Wenxuan, 1975–1982* (Selected Works of Deng Xiaoping, *1975–1982*). Beijing, China: People's Press, 1983.

Dreyer, June T. "China after Tiananmen: The Role of the PLA." *World Policy Journal,* 4 (Fall 1989): 62–71.

_____. "Deng Xiaoping and the Modernization of the Chinese Military." *Armed Forces and Society,* 14, no. 2 (Winter 1988): 647–656.

Fang, Lixiong. *Zhongguoren Zenme la* (What Is Wrong with the Chinese?). Beijing: Red Flag Press, 1992.

Fang, Lizhi. *Bringing Down the Great Wall: Writings on Science, Culture, and Democracy in China.* ed. and trans., James H. Williams. New York: Knopf, 1991.

Fairbank, John King. *China: A New History.* Cambridge, Mass.: Harvard University Press, 1992.

_____. *The United States and China.* 4th ed. Cambridge, Mass.: Harvard University Press, 1983.

Fingar, Thomas, and Paul Blencoe, eds. *China's Quest For Independence: Policy Evolution in the 1970s.* Boulder, Colo.: Westview Press, 1980.

Fitzgerald, C. P. *The Birth of Communist China.* Harmondsworth, U.K.: Penguin, 1964.

Forges, Roger V. Des, Luo Ning, and Wu Yen-bo, eds. *Chinese Democracy and the Crisis of 1989: Chinese and American Reflections.* Albany: State University of New York Press, 1993.

Gold, Thomas B. "Party-State versus Society in China." In Joyce K. Kallgren, ed., *Building a Nation-State: China after Forty Years.* Berkeley, Calif.: University of California, Institute of East Asian Studies, 1990.

_____. "The Resurgence of Civil Society in China," *Journal of Democracy.* vol. 1, no. 1 (Winter 1990): 16–23.

Goodman, D. S. *Groups and Politics in the People's Republic Of China.* Cardiff, U.K.: University of Cardiff Press, 1984.

Hamrin, Carol Lee. *China and the Challenge of the Future: Changing Political Patterns.* Boulder, Colo.: Westview Press, 1990.

Han, Minzhu. *Cries for Democracy.* Princeton, N.J.: Princeton University Press, 1990.

Han, Zi. *Dadi Changshang: Zhgonnanhai Renwu Chengfu Neimu* (The Rise and Fall of the People in Zhongnanhai). Beijing, China: Zhongguo Dadi Press, 1993.

Harding, Harry. *Organizing China: The Problem of Bureaucracy, 1949–1976*. Stanford, Calif.: Stanford University Press, 1981.

_____ . *China's Second Revolution: Reform after Mao*. New York: Brookings Institution, 1987.

He, Baogang. "Democratization: Anti-Democratic and Democratic Elements in the Political Culture of China." *Australian Journal of Political Science*, 27, (1992): 120–137.

Hicks, George, ed. *The Broken Mirror: China after Tiananmen*. New York: St. James Press, 1991.

Ho, Ping-ti, and Tang Tsou, eds. *China in Crisis*. Vol. 1. Chicago, Ill.: University of Chicago Press, 1969.

Howell, Jude. *China Opens Its Doors: The Politics of Economic Transition*. Hemel Hempstead, U.K.: Harvester Wheatsheaf, 1993.

Hsu, Immanuel C. Y. *The Rise of Modern China*. 2nd ed. New York: Oxford University Press, 1975.

Hu, Fuming. "Practice Is the Sole Criterion for Testing Truth." *Guangming Ribao*, May 11, 1978.

Hu, Shun. *Zhongguo Gongchandang de Qishi Nian* (Seventy Years of the Chinese Communist Party). Beijing: CCP history Press, 1991.

Huang, Yasheng. "Origins of China's Pro-Democracy Movement." *Fletcher Forum of World Affairs*, 14 (Winter 1990): 30–46.

Huntington, Samuel P. *The Third Wave: Democratization in the Late Twentieth Century*. Norman: University of Oklahoma Press, 1991.

_____ . "The Goals of Development." In Myron Weiner and Samuel Huntington, eds. *Understanding Political Development*. Boston: Little, Brown and Company, 1987.

Isaak, Alan C. *Scope and Methods of Political Science*. Homewood, Ill.: Dorsey Press, 1985.

Jiang, Zhifeng. *Wangpai chujin de Zhongnanhai Qiaoju* (The Game of Bridge without Trump Cards). San Francisco, Calif.: Democratic China Books Press, 1990.

Joseph, A. William. *The Critique of Ultra-Leftism in China 1958–1981*. Stanford, Calif.: Stanford University Press, 1984.

Joseph, A. William, Christine P. W. Wong, and David Zweig, eds. *New Perspectives on the Cultural Revolution*. Cambridge, Mass.: Harvard University, The Council on East Asian Studies, 1991.

Kane, Anthony J. *China Briefing, 1990*. Boulder, Colo.: Westview Press, 1990.

Ladany, Laszlo. *The Communist Party of China and Marxism, 1921–1985: A Self Portrait*. Stanford, Calif.: Hoover Institution Press, 1988.

Lampton, David M., ed. *Policy Implementation in Post–Mao China*. Berkeley: University of California Press, 1987.

_____ . *The Politics of Medicine in China: The Policy Process, 1949–1977*. Boulder, Colo.: Westview Press, 1977.

Lee, Feigon. *China Rising: The Meaning of Tiananmen*. Chicago, Ill.: Ivan Dee, 1990.

Lee, Hong Yung. *From Revolutionary Cadres to Party Technocrats in Socialist China*. Berkeley : University of California Press, 1991.

Levenson, Joseph R. *Confucian China and Its Modern Fate*. 3 vols. Berkeley.: University of California Press, 1958–1965.

Li, Peter, Steven Mark, and Marjorie H. Li, eds. *Culture and Politics in China: An Anatomy of Tiananmen Square*. New Brunswick, N.J.: Transaction Publishers, 1991.

Li, Rui. *Mao Zedong de Zaonian yu Wannian* (Mao Zedong Young and Old). Guiyang, China: Guizhou People's Press, 1992.

Li, Yong et al. eds. *Wenhua Da Geming zhong de Minren zhi Si* (Deaths of Famous Individuals during the Cultural Revolution). Beijing: Central Nationalities Institute Press, 1993.

_____ . *Wenhau Da Geming zhong de Mingren zhi Yu* (Persecution of Famous Individuals during the Cultural Revolution). Beijing: Central Nationalities Institute Press, 1993.

Liang, Heng, and Judith Shapiro. *Son of the Revolution*. New York: Alfred A. Knopf, 1983.

_____ . *After the Nightmare: A Survivor of the Cultural Revolution Reports on China Today*. New York: Alfred A. Knopf, 1986.

Lieberthal, Kenneth, and David M. Lampton, eds. *Bureaucracy, Politics, and Decision Making in Post–Mao China*. Berkeley : University of California Press, 1992.

Lieberthal, Kenneth, and Michel Oksenberg. *Policy Making in China: Leaders, Structures, and Processes*. Princeton, N.J.: Princeton University Press, 1988.

Liu, Binyan, Ruan Ming, and Xu Gang. *Tell the World: What Happened in China and Why*. Trans. Henry L. Epstein. New York: Pantheon Books, 1989.

Liu, Guoguang. "Socialism Is Not Egalitarianism." *Beijing Review*, 39 (September 28, 1987): 16–18.

Liu, Minghua. *Shiji Xuanfeng: Rencai Da Taowang* (Wind of the Century: The Great Flight of Talents). Chongqing, China: Chongqing University Press, 1993.

Lo, Carlos Wing-Hung. "The Chinese Communist Party's Perception of Crisis and Methods of Crisis Solving during the 1989 Democratic Movement: A Legal Perspective." *Asian Affairs: An American Review* 19 (Summer 1992): 97–120.

Mackerras, Colin, and Amanda Yorke. *The Cambridge Handbook of Contemporary China*. New York: Cambridge University Press, 1991.

Macridis, Roy C. *Modern Political Regimes*. Boston: Little, Brown and Company, 1986.

Madsen, Richard. "The Public Sphere, Civil Society and Moral Community." *Modern China* (April 1993): 183–197.

Magstadt, Thomas M., and Peter M. Schotten. *Understanding Politics: Ideas, Institutions, and Issues*. New York: St. Martin's Press, 1988.

Mancall, Mark. *China at the Center: 300 Years of Foreign Policy*. New York: Free Press, 1984.

McCormick, Barrett L. *Political Reform in Post–Mao China: Democracy and Bureaucracy in a Leninist State*. Berkeley: University of California Press, 1990.

Meisner, Maurice. *Mao's China: A History of the People's Republic*. New York: Free Press, 1977.

Mills, Miriam K., and Stuart S. Nagel, eds. *Public Administration in China*. Westport, Conn.: Greenwood Press, 1993.

Nathan, Andrew J. *China's Crisis: Dilemmas of Reform and Prospects for Democracy*. New York: Columbia University Press, 1990.

_____ . *Chinese Democracy*. New York: Alfred A. Knopf, 1985.

_____ . "A Factional Model of Chinese Politics." *China Quarterly*, no. 53 (January-March 1973): 34–66.

Nee, Victor, and David Mozingo, eds. *State and Society in Contemporary China*. Ithaca, N.Y.: Cornell University Press, 1983.

Ninton, William. *The Great Reversal: The Privatization of China, 1978–1989*. New York: Monthly Review Press, 1990.

O'Donnell, Guillermo, Phillippe C. Schmitter, and Laurence Whitehead, eds. *Transitions from Authoritarian Rule: Prospects for Democracy*. Baltimore: The Johns Hopkins University Press, 1986.

Ogden, Suzanne. *China's Unresolved Issues: Politics, Development, and Culture*. 2nd ed. Englewood Cliffs, N.J.: Prentice Hall, 1992.

Ogden, Suzanne, Kathleen Hartford, Lawrence Sullivan, and David Zweig, eds. *China's Search for Democracy: The Student and Mass Movement of 1989*. Armonk, N.Y.: M. E. Sharpe, 1992.

Oksenberg, Michel, Lawrence R. Sullivan, and Marc Lambert, eds. *Beijing Spring 1989, Confrontation and Conflict: The Basic Documents*. Armonk, N.Y.: M. E. Sharpe, 1990.

Parish, William L. "Factions in Chinese Military Politics." *China Quarterly*, no. 56 (October-December 1973): 667–699.

Perkins, Dwight H. "The Prospects for China's Economic Reforms." In Anthony J. Kane, ed. *China Briefing, 1990*. Boulder, Colo.: Westview Press, 1990.

Perlmutter, Amos. *Modern Authoritarianism: A Comparative Institutional Analysis*. New Haven, Conn.: Yale University Press, 1981.

Perry, Elizabeth J., and Christine Wong, eds. *The Political Economy of Reform in Post-Mao China*. Cambridge, Mass.: Harvard University Press, Council on East Asian Studies, 1985.

Pye, Lucian W. *The Spirit of Chinese Politics*. Cambridge, Mass.: Harvard University Press, 1992.

_____ . "The State and the Individual: An Overview Interpretation," *The China Quarterly* 127 (September 1991): 443–466.

_____ . "Tiananmen and Chinese Political Culture: The Escalation of Confrontation from Moralizing to Revenge." *Asian Survey* 30 (April 1990): 331–347.

_____ . *The Mandarin and the Cadre*. Ann Arbor: University of Michigan Center for Chinese Studies, 1988.

_____ . "Reassessing the Cultural Revolution," *China Quarterly* 108 (December 1986): 597–612.

_____ . *Dynamics of Chinese Politics*. Cambridge, Mass.: Oelgeschlager, Gunn and Hain, 1981.

Pye, Lucian W., and Mary W. Pye. *Asian Power and Politics: The Cultural Dimensions of Authority*. Cambridge, Mass.: Harvard University Press, 1985.

Radin, Charles. "Communism's Longevity Rests on Economy." *Denver Post*, June 13, 1993.

Rozman, Gilbert. *The Chinese Debate about Soviet Socialism, 1978–1985*. Princeton, N.J.: Princeton University Press, 1987.

_____ , ed. *The Modernization of China*. New York: Free Press, 1981.

Schell, Orville. *Discos and Democracy: China in the Throes of Reform*. New York: Pantheon Books, 1988.

Schram, Stuart R. "China after the 13th Congress," *The China Quarterly* 114 (June 1988): 177–197.

_____ . "Economics in Command: Ideology and Policy since the Third Plenum, 1978–1984," *China Quarterly* 99 (September 1984): 417–461.

Shapiro, Judith, and Liang Heng. *Cold Winds, Warm Winds: Intellectual Life in China Today*. Middletown, Conn.: Wesleyan University Press, 1986.

Shue, Vivienne. *The Reach of the State: Sketches of the Chinese Body Politic*. Stanford, Calif.: Stanford University Press, 1988.

Smith, Richard J. *China's Cultural Heritage: The Ch'ing Dynasty*. Boulder, Colo.: Westview Press, 1983.

Solinger, Dorothy J. *China's Transition from Socialism: Statist Legacies and Market Reforms, 1980–1990*. Armonk, N.Y.: M. E. Sharpe, 1993.

Solomon, Richard. *Mao's Revolution and Chinese Political Culture*. Berkeley: University of California Press, 1971.

Spencer, Jonathan D. *The Search for Modern China*. New York: W. W. Norton, 1990.

Su, Shaozhi, et al. "What Will the Year 1989 Tell Us?" In Suzanne Ogden, Kathleen Hartford, Lawrence Sullivan, and David Zweig, eds., *China's Search for Democracy: The Student and Mass Movement of 1989*. Armonk, N.Y.: M. E. Sharpe, 1992.

Su, Xiaokang, and Wang Lusiang. "*He Shang*" (River Elegy) (TV script). Excerpted in *Shonguo Zhi Chun (China Spring)* (January/February 1989): 36–69.

Tang, Buyun, and Yang Huiming. *Zhongguo 1993: Zouchu hundun* (China in 1993: Coming Out of Chaos). Chengdu, China: Sichuan People's Press, 1993.

Teiwes, Frederick C. *Leadership, Legitimacy, and Conflict in China*. Armonk, N.Y.: M. E. Sharpe, 1983.

Terrill, Ross. *China in Our Time: The Epic Saga of the People's Republic from the Communist Victory to Tiananmen Square and Beyond*. New York: Simon & Schuster, 1992.

Thurston, Anne. *Enemies of the People: The Ordeal of the Intellectuals in China's Great Cultural Revolution*. New York, 1987.

Truman, David. *The Governmental Process*. 2nd ed. New York: Alfred A. Knopf, 1971.

Tsou, Tang. *The Cultural Revolution and Post-Mao Reforms: A Historical Perspective*. Chicago, Ill.: The University of Chicago Press, 1986.

Wakeman, Frederic, Jr. *The Fall of Imperial China*. New York: Free Press, 1975.

Wang, Baoliang, Chen Guoyao and Liu Mingpuo. *Zhongguo Zai Sikao: '92 Da Xieshi* (China Rethinking: Fact Report of 1992 Portrait). Beijing, China: People's Press, 1992.

Wang, James C.F. *Contemporary Chinese Politics: An Introduction*. 4th ed. Englewood Cliffs, NJ: Prentice Hall, 1992.

_____. *The Cultural Revolution in China: An Annotated Bibliography*. New York: Garland Publishing, 1976.

Wasserstrom, Jeffrey N., and Elizabeth J. Perry, eds. *Popular Protests and Political Culture in Modern China: Learning from 1989*. Boulder, Colo.: Westview Press, 1992.

Wei, Hongyun. *A Modern History of China: 1919–1949*. Harbin, China: Harbin People's Press, 1982.

Wei, Jingsheng. "The Fifth Modernization: Democracy and Etc." *Beijing zhi Chun* (Beijing Spring) 5 (October 1993).

Wen, Yu. *Zhongguo Zuohuo* (China's Leftist Peril). Beijing: Zhaohua Press, 1993.

White, Lynn. *Policies of Chaos: The Organizational Causes of Violence in China's Cultural Revolution*. Princeton, N.Y.: Princeton University Press, 1989.

Wilson, Jeanne. "Labor Policy in China: Reform and Retrogression." *Problems of Communism* 39 (September-October 1990): 44–65.

Wittfogel, Karl A. *Oriental Despotism*. New Haven, Conn.: Yale University Press, 1957.

Womack, Brantly, ed. *Contemporary Chinese Politics in Historical Perspective*. Cambridge: Cambridge University Press, 1991.

Yan, Jiaqi, and Gao Gao. *Zhongguo Wenge Shinian Shi* (A History of China's Ten-Year Cultural Revolution). Beijing: China Studies Press, 1986.

Yang, Jiang. *Six Chapters from My Life "Downunder."* Seattle: University of Washington Press, 1984.

Yee, Lee, ed. *The New Realism: Writings from China after the Cultural Revolution*. New York: Hipporence Books, 1983.

Yu, Xiguang, Jing Li, and Jianzhong Ni. *Dachao Xinqi: Deng Xiaoping Nanxun Qianqian Houhou* (Spring Tide: Before and after Deng Xiaoping's Tour in Southern China). Beijing: Chinese Broadcast and Television Press, 1992.

Yuan, Zhixin. *Guo zhong zhi Guo* (State within a State). Guangzhou, China: Jinan University Press, 1992.

Zarrow, Peter. *Anarchism and Chinese Political Culture*. New York: Columbia University Press, 1990.

Zhang, Ming, and Le Qun, eds. *Wenhua De Geming de Mingren zhi Si* (Reflections of Famous Individuals during the Cultural Revolution). Beijing: Central Nationalities Institute Press, 1993.

Zhang, Weixuan, and Liu Wuyi. *Gongheguo Fengyun Sishi Nian* (Forty Eventful Years of the People's Republic). 2 vols. Beijing: China University of Political Science and Law, 1989.

Zhao, Cong. *Wenge Yundong Licheng Shulue* (An Outline history of the Cultural Revolution). Hong Kong: Youlian Research Institute, 1975.

Zweig, David. *Agrarian Radicalism in China, 1968–1981*. Cambridge, Mass.: Harvard University Press, 1989.

Index

About the Authors

JIE CHEN is Assistant Professor of Political Science at the University of Wisconsin–River Falls. He is the author of *Ideology in U.S. Foreign Policy* (Praeger, 1994).

PENG DENG is Assistant Professor of History at High Point University. His first book in English was *China's Crisis and Revolution Through American Lenses* (1994).